SEA-FISHING FROM THE SHORE

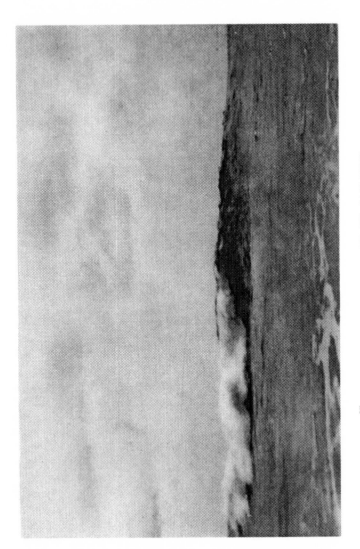

THE ROLLER BEHIND WHICH THE BIG BASS LURK.

SEA-FISHING FROM THE SHORE

BY
A. R. HARRIS CASS, M.B.E.

Author of
"THE SALT WIND FROM THE WEST," etc.
Contributor to
" ANGLING," the " FISHING GAZETTE," etc.

HERBERT JENKINS LIMITED
3 DUKE OF YORK STREET
ST. JAMES'S LONDON S.W.1 ❀ ❀

A
HERBERT
JENKINS'
BOOK

First printing 1940

Printed in Great Britain by Wyman & Sons Ltd., London, Reading and Fakenham.

FOREWORD

WHEN I read the manuscript of this book shortly after the outbreak of war, I found it both interesting and informative. Are these not two of the best reasons for a further expansion of the Angler's library ? I think so.

There can never be too many books which help to unravel the mysteries of the greatest of sports. The author has knowledge born of long experience —and an easy pen. If you are interested in fishing from the seashore you will do well to pass quickly from these ruminations to the helpful pages which follow. I am honoured to pen these introductory lines to a book which deals with a phase of sea-fishing which has been sadly neglected and which, under war conditions, has gained greatly in importance.

E. MARSHALL-HARDY,
Editor of *Angling*.

Marlow, Bucks,
9th May, 1940.

PREFACE

ALTHOUGH originally intended for those who desire some information regarding rod fishing from the seashore, this little work contains much that should be known by every visitor to seaside resorts.

     *   *   *   *

I am indebted to E. Marshall-Hardy for his spontaneous offer to illustrate this work and write a foreword thereto. The phrase " thank you " is very simple, but in this instance it conveys my deep appreciation for a labour of love.

A. R. HARRIS CASS.

CONTENTS

ILLUSTRATIONS

FROM PHOTOGRAPHS TAKEN BY THE AUTHOR

CHAPTER I

WHY FISH ?

A MONGST the many quaint questions that have been put to me, from time to time, has been the hardy annual, " Why do you fish ? " For the information of those who have not ventured the query personally, but who, no doubt, would like to know the answer, I will state at once that my reasons are threefold, namely recreation, sport, and a pleasing reward for my efforts.

Living within a mile of the sea, and, rod in hand, visiting the shore most weeks throughout the year, I am constantly interviewed by strangers who usually preface their remarks by the interrogation " Fishing ? " Not wishing to be rude I invariably reply in the affirmative, although I sometimes wonder what the questioner could possibly imagine I was doing otherwise. During the peak of the holiday season, however, the inquiries are more persistent, and at times somewhat embarrassing, especially if they are born of mere inquisitiveness, though, like all other anglers, I am only too pleased to impart any and all information to *bona fide*

13

fishing brethren, whether actual or potential, for
that is a real pleasure as the joy is mutual. As an
example of the reverse influence let me mention
an experience of a few years ago. I arrived on
one hot afternoon in August, at my favourite spot
on the shore, glad to see a dear old friend already
there. He was a man of substance who enjoyed a
stretch of salmon rights on a near-by river, and
out in the bay his steam yacht, riding at anchor,
made a charming picture. He was just crazy on
fishing, and was completely happy if he had his
rod, whether throwing a fly over the river, away
miles out deep-sea fishing, or trying his luck from
the seashore. He never seemed to grow up, retain-
ing, year after year, the happy outlook that possessed
him when, as a boy, he used to catch " tiddlers " in
a stream. I have seen him lose a fine fish after a
real tussle, seen him break the top of his favourite
rod, and been with him when other adverse vicissi-
tudes, so peculiar at times to anglers, have beset
him ; but he had always accepted those trials in a
happy state of optimism. I had never known him
perturbed or ill-tempered : hence when I greeted
him, I was astonished to hear him say, " I am
irritable." Looking round to see whether I could
trace the cause for the effect, he laughed and
intimated " Nothing like that. No. It was like
this. When George dropped me, I told him to
return with the car at four o'clock. I made up my
mind for a couple of hours' peaceful fishing, but

A FAR-FLUNG ESTUARY WITH DEEP WATER CHANNEL.

within the first half hour a procession of trippers passed by, and each individual stopped, inquiring ' Fishing ? ' The same old inane question got me down at last ; then when a couple—a girl and a fellow obviously on a hike—stood by me, and the girl trilled ' Fishing ? ' I was real bored, and said nothing. The girl repeated the word, and as that did not produce the desired attention, the fellow came close, cupped his hands, and bawled in my ear ' Fishing ? ' I turned round, looked them up and down in rather a cavalier manner, and replied, ' Yes. Why ? ' They were taken back, and the fellow rejoined meekly, ' Oh ! Just curiosity, you know,' adding ' It's not unusual to ask a fishermen whether he has had any luck.' I felt that I had been a trifle unkind, and replied, ' Yes, I am aware of that, but there is another side to be considered. You are evidently hiking ; now suppose, as you walked down the village street, everybody said to you " Hiking ? " You would feel a bit weary of the incessant repetition ; so it is with me.' They both laughed, and the fellow said, ' Righto, I tumble. Anyhow I hope that you will have good luck.' ' Thanks, and I trust that you will have an enjoyable hike,' I replied ; and they passed on gleefully. However, I'm glad that you have come, you will be able to share the interruptions." We soon settled down to enjoy our recreation.

In recollecting the incident, and contemplating upon the seashore during the holiday months, I cannot help thinking how much many of the visitors miss, especially those who select haunts which accommodate a sparse number of seasonal families : there I witness the same ritual day after day. Dotted along the sands, small groups comprising usually father, mother, and their offspring take up their positions for the morning or afternoon. Father reads his paper, mother is lost in a book, meanwhile the little ones dig and build. Before long for lack of something better to do, father prospects in the sand for small stones with which to throw at a shell or something else that has caught his eye. If the shore be a pebbly one, you may calculate that the members of three groups out of every four employ their time by throwing pebbles into the sea. Strange what a state of ennui seems to descend quickly on these summer migrants. True they enjoy a rest from their ordinary every-day toils, but I venture to think that a change of occupation would prove more beneficial. Should an angler appear on the shore all eyes will turn on him, and every time that he reels in, his spectators will be expecting to see a fish. They are keenly interested. Should he produce the anticipated finny one, he will be besieged by an excited gallery, and the questions put to him will be many and comprehensive. Probably some of the fathers will be so fired by enthusiasm that their inquiries will take a more concrete form, and after a visit to the nearest tackle shop, will blossom out the following

day as fully equipped anglers—anglers not only
for that brief holiday, but anglers for many, many
subsequent years. What a pity that they, and
countless others, had not realized the possibilities
of shore angling before starting on their trip to the
seaside. It is sad to think how much fun by the
sea so many have missed owing solely to want of
knowledge. Not only fun, but inspiring recreation,
and something, perchance, to recount again and
again : something that will not only live in memory,
but bring a thrill every time it is recalled : something to make personal history. Further when
next they sojourn by the sea, they will not be
included in the company who ask silly questions.
At times I have been truly amazed at the ignorance
regarding fish, displayed by obviously intelligent
people, men who would have no difficulty in making
a selection from a menu, but who, having never
seen their choice in its natural state, would be at a
loss to recognize it when it was caught. In a fishmonger's shop they could, without hesitation,
indicate kippers, cured haddock and mackerel, but
to divide " flats " into their many classes they would
be at a loss, while the other specimens would occasion
them similar trouble to describe. The amusing
aspect is that these city men who, in other walks of
life, would never forgive themselves if they thought
that they had been guilty of a *faux pas*, unblush-
ingly lay themselves open to ridicule when they
descend on a shore angler.

Now for fishing as a sport. With a full-blooded drive, to send a ball out of the ground, for a six; to hole in one; to breast the tape after a strenuous sprint; to break through, flash along the line, dodge the full back, and then grass the ball behind the goal posts, these and similar outstanding incidents will produce a thrill on recollection, but believe me, for I have sampled them all, not one will compare with the gasp that accompanies the memory of the capture of a big bass. Looking back a few decades, I remember as though it were but yesterday, my first noteworthy fish. Standing on a rocky ledge, in the vicinity of a Cornish holiday resort, I was wondering how much longer the incoming spring tide, with a strong westerly breeze behind it, would permit me to occupy my precarious position. Every now and again a large wave would swirl along the side of the slippery ledge, sometimes boiling over the edge in an ominous manner, and sending up lumps of water that splashed me with warning thumps. I was using float tackle, and in the waning light of a late September evening I experienced much trouble in following the movements of the piece of dark coloured cork that one minute rode the crest of the wave, and the next minute had disappeared in the trough. Suddenly the cork turned over mysteriously, and then dived. Instinctively I struck, although my first surmise was that I had fouled some drifting weed, but in a split second I received the unmistakable ultimatum of a hooked fish. The line flew off my reel, and the fight commenced. For the first few seconds I was on the defensive, the heavy waters lapped my thigh boots, reminding me of the quickly rising tide, and I hurriedly backed to find a safer stance. I knew that, without doubt, something big and strong was playing a game of give and take with me. Was the tussle with merely one of the out-size dog-fish that frequent that part of the coast, I conjectured with feelings of chagrin. No : when I had reduced the heaving line considerably, I saw in a green-making roller the welcome glint and form of a fine bass, just a glimpse of him before he submerged. As I reeled in, played out ; raised and lowered the point of my rod, I looked round in apprehension. I was alone, and my anxiety was how to land so big a fish in such awkward conditions. As wave followed wave, the water was over the ledge one time, and almost instantly the level had fallen two or three feet : the edges of the reef were sharp, and would quickly saw through a taut line. I had never accounted for a bass of more than four pounds, therefore I thought to lose this one would be a dire calamity. When I commenced to think that the duel would never end, the pull on the line eased : steadily I wound in, he came nearer and nearer without a struggle, then, timing a rising wave to a nicety, I slithered the beauty over the wet rocks. Immediately he seemed to be endowed with a fresh life, and when I saw him springing about, probably in the hope of regaining the sea, I threw myself full length on him, clasping him in a firm if not altogether affectionate embrace. Quickly my fingers were in his gills, and as I held him aloft, a round of hand clapping greeted my ears. Some old " salts," enjoying their evening leisure on a jetty above me, had witnessed the battle, and signified their delight whole-heartedly at the conquest. Later when I had collected my gear and repaired to the local butcher to weigh in, I was delighted to learn that my specimen was credited with a few ounces over eleven pounds. Since that memorable evening I have tried to beat my best, but without success. However a " sport " never says die, so perhaps the day will come when I shall reckon with a heavier fish. If you are new to the game you will, like enthusiasts in all other directions, not be satisfied until you have succeeded in establishing a record, if not for the country, at least for yourself ; and thus so much for sport.

The last reason which, I suggested, caused me to fish, is to obtain a reward commensurate with my endeavours. When I obtain, for bait, a mackerel straight from the sea, I marvel at its wonderful beauty, and I question whether anything more lovely has been yielded by the deep. Stiff as a blade of steel and full of colour it rightly deserves admiration. On the day following, however, what a change has occurred ; gone are the iridescent tints, and the body feels like a lump of putty.

When I catch fish for the table I like it to be served on the same day, and what a delicious flavour it offers. When you have been successful with your rod, and you taste the results, you will be exuberant in your praise. You will know that you are eating something worth while ; and the members of your family who, with you, have enjoyed the repast, will urge you to repeat your fishing expedition at an early date, and will pray for a fitting termination to your labours.

CHAPTER II

IF you, as a tyro, should be contemplating a trial of your skill with your rod, you will naturally desire to know what kinds of fish you may expect to encounter. The one that is outstanding, and the one for which every sea angler makes a bid, is the bass, both for its fighting qualities and its table value. Although it is allied to the perch family, its shape, and its colourings of slate back with silvery sides and belly, cause it to resemble a salmon, especially when its dorsal fin is not raised : hence for this reason it is frequently described as a salmon bass. It evinces its game spirit even when only a few ounces in weight. At that period it roves in shoals, and is then known as school bass. Later, when it matures, it reaches a goodly weight : one of six or seven pounds is not uncommon, while occasionally beach anglers have been successful with some of ten or a dozen pounds. Once a friend of mine, fishing from the shore, caught a specimen of fifteen pounds, six ounces : this held the record for some time. Fish of a large size will put up a

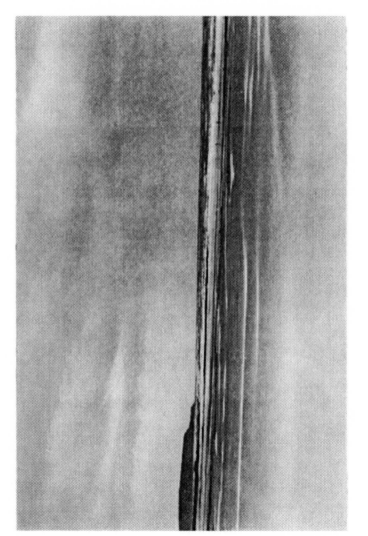

MILES AND MILES OF SANDY SHORE FOR FLAT-FISH.

terrific battle, and the angler needs all his resource to avoid loss, particularly if a heavy sea is running. The dorsal fin is prickly, and can inflict a nasty cut ; therefore when removing a hook from a bass the angler will be well advised to use an old towel or rag with which to hold the fish.

The most probable fish to reward the efforts of the shore angler are " flats." These comprise plaice, flounders, dabs, soles and brill. I give these in the " order of running," in other words according to the prospect of catching them. I have included the sole and the brill in the list, but they cannot be regarded as in-shore fish. Flounders and dabs are to be met where the beach is sandy, especially in the vicinity of estuaries and harbours. Plaice seem to be fairly generally distributed round the coast where the bottom is composed of sand. Although the " flats " referred to do not attain a large size, and do not provide much of a fight, they are very welcome for their edible qualities, and a fish of from a pound and a half to two pounds in weight will supply four delicious fillets.

If the shore angler is fishing where rocks and reefs abound, he will stand a fair chance of connecting with pollock. These fish run to a good size, ten to twelve pounds being not unusual, though of course smaller ones of two or three pounds are more general. The small fry of a few ounces, however, seem to congregate in harbours. If the angler is fishing from a ledge of rocks he will find that a large pollock can put up a very stiff contest, reserving its chief challenge for the minute when it is almost within range of the gaff.

Although grey mullet are occasionally caught from the shore, they cannot be regarded as a reasonable possibility. In the first place they prefer brackish waters, and secondly they are unobliging fish even there, so that the only means of dealing with them effectually is to set out on a special mission, suitably equipped, to angle solely for them. I do not wish, therefore, to create hope concerning grey mullet as a shore catch, but in the chapter devoted to " When to use float tackle " I shall have some remarks to make concerning these shy fish.

When the herrings arrive in the late autumn, and onwards, there are opportunities in abundance for hooking codling from the beach : in fact a cod of respectable weight will not hesitate to take a well-baited hook.

Allcock's
" Little Witch "
Spinner

" When the corn is in the stook, the mackerel are in shore " is a familiar phrase near some parts of the coast, and at that time the last of the summer holiday-makers are still enjoying the seaside. Every day then the mackerel boats are busily reaping the harvest of the sea, while the pleasure boats are fully employed in taking out small parties for a few hours' mackerel whiffing. Should I be using a rod from the shore during that period my many inquirers will want to know either if I am fishing for mackerel, or whether mackerel can be caught from the beach. I am afraid that I cannot recommend this form of shore fishing as within the accepted meaning of that class of sport, as a practically motionless baited hook lying on or near the bottom would not interest a mackerel. I have caught mackerel from the shore, but only by means of a " Little Witch " spinner.

With ordinary shore fishing you will experience disappointments as well as success. For instance when perhaps your patience is becoming exhausted owing to lack of business, you may receive a good and hearty bang on your line. " At last " you say cheerfully, and proceed to gather in the spoil. Your line tells the tale of something big as you reel in quickly, feeling alternately its slackness, and strong pull. You know, by experience, that a lump of heavy seaweed would produce merely a sickening drag, so you anticipate the conclusion with glee, though you may feel a bit suspicious concerning the absence of the usual vim at the end of the line. Still you hope for the best and carry on. Eventually the mouth of your prey comes in view. Speedily you reel the capture beyond the breaking waves. No need to look twice, you certainly have brought the fish in securely. A really big dog-fish. I won't try to express what

25

you think. Perhaps you will merely regret the loss of a nice piece of bait, and seek comfort in the knowledge that the absence of sport has been due to everything else having been frightened away by that wretched creature. However, be careful in handling the brute, as it can be dangerous.

Should your position be adjacent to where the waves play on rocks, do not expect that every healthy bite that is registered is the work of either a bass or a pollock, otherwise you will be disillusioned. Near those rocks is the haunt of the wrasse. That fish has no compunction in swallowing your bait, and will come to hand with scarcely a flick of its tail. It may be a gorgeous fish upon which to look, but it is only fit to use as bait for the lobster pots, though I recollect an old farmer in Cornwall swearing by baked wrasse, and imploring me to give him any that I caught.

In rocky areas there is always the possibility of a conger engaging your attention, and though usually the size of these somewhat rare inshore feeders, during daylight hours, does not exceed half a dozen pounds, the likelihood must not be ruled out of a specimen of considerable weight leaving its deep sea quarters in search of a delicacy thrown up by the pounding rollers. If you hook one of the big kind, and succeed in pulling it ashore, be prepared for trouble, and treat the long slashing tail with caution, for it is capable of causing damage. There are many stories concerning the power of a

conger's tail, and I was amused by a happening
that occurred recently near a Devonshire fishing
cove. An old sailor was out in his boat, hand lining,
and after a not very remunerative morning, he
found at length that he was into something noteworthy. After a hefty pull he brought the head
of a huge conger level with the gunwale : so far,
but no farther. Every time that he strove for
mastery, he merely caused the boat to rock, and
he concluded that the fish had found a good
anchorage in the dark depths. Ultimately when
he was nearly tired of his unavailing labours, he
altered his position so as to work from a different
angle. As he did so he saw that the tail of the
conger was coiled over the opposite gunwale.

If you select a day that does not provide you
with the luck for which you hope, do not despair,
but take comfort from the words of an old friend of
mine. He and I were enjoying a morning on the
shore, when a stranger stopped to have a word with
us : departing, the stranger remarked, " I can't
for the life of me understand how you fellows can
be so patient." My friend looked at me for a few
minutes, smiled and said, " No : he does not see
what you and I observe." Those words " What
you observe " may be regarded as an apt com-
pendium of the many joys of angling. The mere
spoil of the sport is not the only pleasure. You
may be cognisant of the diversions that abound
along the river bank, and may think that the sea

and the shore are devoid of similar attractions. If so, you are mistaken, for nature is always ready to unfold her secrets to everyone who is interested in them. Apart from a jumping fish, the flurry of a shoal, or the antics of a gull that, to smash a crab, or to open a mussel shell, carries its victim aloft, and lets it drop on the rocks, there are many other incidents that are not so ordinary, but which are most fascinating to lovers of wild life.

One afternoon when the fish did not seem to be attracted by my bait, I noticed, not more than twenty yards out, a porpoise suddenly appear. Instead of its leisurely roll being performed, its behaviour signified something out of the common, when, like a torpedo, it sped through the water, keeping close inshore ; then, turning, it tore in the reverse direction. Arriving opposite the spot where I was standing, it headed straight in the direction of the beach. For a second, not knowing what possessed the creature, I surveyed the safety margin of a few feet between me and the edge of the break-ing waves. When the frantic sea pig seemed almost certain to run aground, a fine salmon leapt into the air, and its pursuer slowed up, turned, and made off seawards.

On the same afternoon my attention was claimed by a gull that was acting mysteriously on the bank of the close-by estuary. At first I thought that the bird was shaking a piece of ribbon seaweed, but further scrutiny disclosed the fact that an eel of about fifteen inches in length was providing the attraction. Gradually the eel would slither down the muddy slope, but when the water was nearly reached the gull charged, jabbed the retreating one by the head, and tossed it up the bank. Again and again these proceedings were enacted, until finally the eel was past the squirming stage. Then the gull, starting with the head of its victim, slowly swallowed the prize, every now and again pausing in its task. When the meal was completed the gull, with a bulging crop resembling a huge goitre, took to the air and drifted out to sea.

Therefore do not take angling too seriously, but enjoy its many attendant pleasures, for there is always something worth noting apart from the feel of the line.

CHAPTER III

TACKLE

SOME years ago I was spending a fishing holiday in a Devonshire favourite resort, and as my luck was in, most days I returned, with a good bag, to the hotel where I was staying, much to the satisfaction of the management, the guests, and myself. One day a doting mother informed me that her young son would be coming down to join her for a portion of his school holidays ; she had written to him telling him of my exploits, and as he was " just potty," she said, on beach fishing, would I be so kind as to supply her with a list of the things that her son would need to catch fish, where she could purchase them, and what they would cost. I compiled a detailed statement which I considered would prove suitable, but to my astonishment the good lady intimated that her son would not be satisfied with that outfit ; he would want one costing ten times the amount which I had suggested. I mention the incident merely as indicative of what may be spent on the necessary articles. Like with most other sports, the outlay can be governed by the individual purse.

The first item to be considered is the rod : this may be obtained for shillings or pounds. For the beginner I recommend one not too costly. I purchased an inexpensive one nearly half a century

A useful agate lined end ring for light rods

This excellent Allcock end ring is porcelain lined and well protected for use with heavier rods

A good " stand off " agate lined intermediate ring, for use with light rods

A well designed protected porcelain Allcock intermediate ring, for use with heavier rods

ago, and though my collection has grown considerably since then, I still rely on my first love when heavy seas are running, especially if the ground swell has torn up a lot of weed. For general utility purposes I am of opinion that a stout two-piece one, giving a total length of eight feet, cannot be beaten. Of course for light or specialized forms of fishing other rods are obtainable, but as a start try the one which I have mentioned. If possible select one with an agate end ring. You will be more than compensated for the slight extra cost. The ordinary porcelain end rings are quite good providing that you do not drop your rod on rocks or pebbles. On a sandy beach you will not run the risk of a broken ring, but the catastrophe is ever present elsewhere, and a spoilt expedition due to a cracked ring is more than the average angler can tolerate. When making your purchase assemble the rod, fit the reel which you choose, and try the weight and balance. Satisfy yourself that you have picked out the rod that you want, for you are selecting a friend for life. If you are unable to obtain your requirements locally, do not be afraid to send to one of the many reputable tackle dealers, stating in detail what you desire. Many times I have had to rely on obtaining my wants by post, and I have always been completely satisfied, and my experience has been that tackle dealers take a personal and friendly interest in their angling customers.

I have referred to a reel ; now for a few words of

A REEF: THE HOME OF POLLOCK AND WRASSE.

advice concerning that important article. There are numerous makes on the market, but for the beginner I suggest one of the following two : a wooden one on the Nottingham principle with a strong brass star back, brass-lined, optional check and winged nut, diameter four inches ; or a bakelite one, of similar size, with a spindle drag operated by a bakelite knob. Both these patterns are simple in design, and will stand up to hard usage. On a sandy shore, however careful you may be, the way that sand will work into any mechanism is remarkable ; you pick up particles both on your fingers and on your line, therefore periodically you will be wise to take your reel to pieces and wipe out with a rag the offending stuff. Hence a reel that can be easily dismantled and reassembled at home, or quickly attended to in case of trouble on the beach, is the one to win your favour.

Now we will consider the line. There are many really good kinds on offer. Any one of these will suit you. The only specifications that matter are that the line should be composed of twisted flax, dark green, fifty or sixty yards in length, and with a breaking strain of say thirty pounds. Not that you are going to catch a fish of those proportions, but you have to remember that salt water, sand friction, and the toll of sharp stones have a deleterious effect on the best of lines, while a plunging fish, aided by the crashing waves, can put up a breaking strain considerably greater than the mere weight of the victim.

There is no point in thinking that the line is too thick, because sea conditions are totally different to those that obtain in fresh water angling. I remember when once fishing with heavy gear for big bass, I was pestered by a number of sharp, elusive bites ; becoming exasperated I held the line exceptionally tight, and struck almost at the exact second as the next bite came along. Reeling in, I found that I had, with a large hook, lipped a baby whiting of about two ounces in weight. So do not hesitate to use a stout line.

The next item, to come under our deliberations, is the cast. Assuming that you do not wish to make your casts, you can obtain suitable ones with

Hooks, actual size

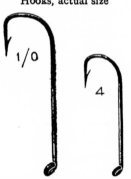

1/0

4

For Bass   For " flats "

a loop at each end. Select those described as " stout," and one yard in length. The hooks, to use with these casts, are described as being suitable for fresh or salt water angling, and are known as rustproof bronzed finish, mounted to specially selected and tested single gut. The sizes best to meet general requirements are number 1/0 for bass, and number 4 for " flats." The real reason for the different sizes is that a smaller bait is sufficient for " flats " and also for school bass, while for large bass, also heavy pollock, a bigger hook is essential.

The most economical method, however, of preparing casts is to make your own, and incidentally the task is interesting. If you are using specially made casts and mounted hooks, a perusal of the following will aid you in assembling your purchase. For the home-made pattern, obtain a coil of stout gut substitute, and a supply of eyed hooks of the sizes previously suggested.

For large bass, take a length of gut substitute of four feet and another piece of one foot. I stipulate four feet to allow plenty of margin for making the knots at both ends. Soak the gut in warm water, until it is soft and pliable. Attach the smaller piece to the hook, and then tie this to the long piece about eighteen inches from what will be the bottom end, using only one hook for this kind of fishing.

For " flats " and school bass proceed in the same way, but using two hooks. In attaching these mounted hooks to the trace, the lower one should

35

be a foot from the end, and the higher one about two feet away from where the bottom one is fastened, the idea being that the two hooks shall

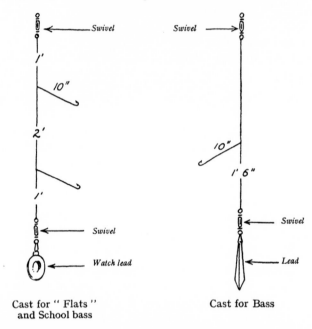

Cast for " Flats "
and School bass

Cast for Bass

not foul each other. Allowing for the gut used in tying the knots, you will see that these measurements will prove adequate.

A supply of box brass swivels—say $1\frac{1}{4}$ inches—is essential. Although one, at that end of the trace to be attached to the line, will suffice, I use one at each end of the trace, as I like if necessary to change the lead quickly.

You may be in doubt concerning the method of tying the gut, so I will describe a knot that I have adhered to with no failures for many years. Before you try it with the gut, experiment with a piece of string, and to satisfy yourself that the knot is a success put the hook through the ring of a key in a door, then pull and jerk energetically. If the knot will stand that treatment, you may pronounce it as being secure.

With one hand, thread the gut through the eye of the hook, with the other hand holding the barbed end of the hook : make a loop on the near side of the shank, give three turns of the gut round the loop and the shank, thread through the turn nearest the eye and through the eye. Pull both long and short ends of the gut, taking care that the turn

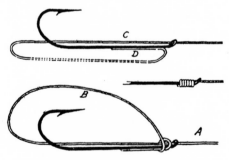

To attach gut or gut substitute to an eyed-hook

nearest the eye is the last to tighten : that last turn may be regarded as the locking one. This may sound a trifle complicated, but after two or three attempts, the effort will offer no difficulty. I use the same style of knot to attach the gut to the swivels, and also to attach the mounted hooks to the trace. In performing the latter operation I make an ordinary single loop tie in the trace where required, and thread the hook-gut through the loop, then knot the hook-gut, and pull.

The last consideration of your line is the lead. The two patterns that have pleased me most are the ones known as the watch shaped lead, and the torpedo lead. The latter, as its name signifies, will take your line out excellently, and it is very suitable for pebbly and stony bottoms which are likely to foul the watch type. For sandy beaches, where you want to establish a hold, the watch type answers well.

Regarding the weight of the lead, I find that two ounces are ample for ordinary seas, but if there is much swell then I resort to four ounces. At times after a short period of fishing, the wind freshens, and the lighter lead fails to function, then the advantages of a swivel are apparent. The connection of the lead by means of a bit of line can be speedily undone, and the lead changed ; whereas even if the gut is soft enough, it is more difficult than line to unknot and re-tie : while in case of need you do not mind sacrificing an odd piece of line, but you would think twice before shortening your gut trace.

A good plan is to make up several traces to be used according to the conditions that prevail when you reach the shore ; by such means you are able to commence work immediately on arrival, whatever the sea says.

There are many gadgets which you may like to try by the way of adjuncts to the trace, but on these you must form your own opinion, as there is no hard and fast rule as to their value or otherwise.

You will observe that I laid down a specified length for the cast. Probably you wonder why. The answer is simple. Allowing for the swivels and the lead, the total length is just over three feet. When your gear is assembled, you will find t hat with the line swivel well clear of the rod's top ring, the lead is about level with your hands holding the rod. In casting you will thus appreciate that you have an ideal length to swing, and your line is free of all obstructions, so that it can travel smoothly through the rings from the reel. I have at times observed anglers using a longer cast, and expecting the line swivel to pass without hindrance through the top ring. Occasionally I have noticed disastrous results as a sequel.

You will, of course, require a fishing bag in which to carry your gear. One useful article to in clude in your outfit is a disgorger, for at times the catch has a nasty trick of getting the hook far down and well embedded.

A gaff is necessary if you intend to fish from

rocks, but this aid may be dispensed with when angling from the beach.

After enjoying your first thrills, you will probably wish to increase your tackle, and try out various ingenious devices. A fishing catalogue from one of the many tackle firms will be of great interest to you, particularly on the days when the weather says " No " to your pre-arranged angling trips.

CHAPTER IV

BAIT

POSSIBLY the most important factor concerning sea angling is bait. To name the various kinds of suitable lures is easy, but the beginner wishes to be informed of something more comprehensive than mere names. When I took up shore fishing, I made inquiries regarding the correct bait to use, and the mention of several alternatives left me with a hazy idea of where to obtain the necessaries, and how to use them when procured. I was residing inland at that time, and the spoils of the sea and shore were unknown to me. If you live at the seaside these mysteries are revealed to you, and the local sea angler does not require informative instructions ; he is well versed in all these interesting details, but the inlander who depends solely on his holidays to enable him to enjoy the coast, wants a ready means of reference and assistance.

Of the many baits, perhaps the best all-round one is the crab, especially as it answers well everywhere and in all circumstances. Crabs used on the hook may be divided into two classes, namely

" soft " and " peelers." The soft crab is one that has shed its shell and has not again grown a new one, while the " peeler " is one that has developed a new shell, but of such a thin texture that it can be removed by your fingers. Both these varieties are found in estuaries and muddy creeks where they are sojourning during the period of growing their fresh covering. In some estuaries quite a business is done in obtaining these crabs, and some " merchants " who send away their catch every day to various angling districts, speak of their yearly harvest in terms of a ton. The usual method employed by these professional bait procurers is to put down old pantiles duly painted with the owner's initials. Under these tiles the crabs take shelter, and after every tide a visit is made by the " merchant " to these simple traps to collect the spoil. The amateur generally depends on the use of some old tins and jars, or he will make a pilgrimage along a muddy inlet at low water, and will find his requirements by turning over weed-covered stones. In most seaside resorts where sea angling is indulged in to any great extent, a local angling association exists, and the visitor cannot do better than to get into touch with that body. If crabs are unobtainable locally the address of a bait " merchant " can usually be ascertained from the secretary of the association.

What is somewhat remarkable about these crabs is that one estuary produces perfect bait specimens, fat and fleshy, whereas other estuaries, in the same district, offer a very poor lot of watery things that are practically useless for the hook.

Having acquired your crabs the next thing is how to use them. The soft kind may provide suitable hook covering either whole or halved or quartered. The size of the crab and the size of the hook being the deciding elements. In any case there is no need to remove either the claws or the legs of the soft species. With " peelers," size is the determining point also, though, as collectors rarely trouble about small ones, those at your disposal generally have to be bisected. A satisfactory way to perform this operation is to place the crab upside down on a board, then using a sharp knife divide it into halves, or quarters as the case may be. The shell should be fingered off, and the legs and claws removed : the legs are useless, but crack the shell of the claws and the inside will, either separately or in pairs, make a tasty bait.

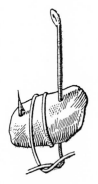

A good plan to retain the crab on the hook is to tie a couple of turns of worsted round the bait. The loosening action due to the chafe of the sands and sea, also sucking " bites " can thus be overcome.

A couple of turns of worsted will keep a piece of crab on the hook

The price of these crabs, whether purchased

from the collector, or from an obliging boatman, is in the neighbourhood of a shilling a dozen. That number is ample for several excursions.

To keep the crabs alive, put some sand that is damp with sea water, and a small quantity of ordinary seaweed in a wooden box : be careful, however, after introducing the crabs to their new home to place a cover over the top of the box, otherwise the creatures will escape. If the box is kept in a cool, shady position, the crabs should remain alive for at least a week.

You will probably use a discarded household tin, with a cover that you have perforated, in which to carry the crabs when you go fishing. On reaching the shore let some sea water percolate into the tin, and keep it there for several minutes, so that the crabs can enjoy a drink.

The next bait in order of merit, in my opinion, is the lug-worm. On a sandy shore you may expect to find these. Look, at low tide, for worm casts similar to those which you see on a lawn. Lug-worms, like all other living things, have their particular haunts. I could show you a beach some three miles in extent, and as you walked along it, you would not see a trace of a lug-worm, but at one end, for a length of about a hundred yards, the sand is teeming with casts. So do not be disappointed if by a casual inspection, you fail to discover evidence of the existence of these worms.

As with all other acts, there is a knack in digging

A POINT THAT ALLOWS IN AND OUT TIDE FISHING.

for lug-worms, and the secret in using a spade is to send it down straight, and to its full length ; but note this, you cannot dig too quickly, nor turn over the spadeful too rapidly. If your actions are " slow motion " you may bring up half a worm here and there, but all the other worms will be down well away, for these lug-worms are very active in disappearing in the depths.

Although this form of bait may be used anywhere, and at any time, it is most deadly when tried on a sandy beach, as it is the natural food of foraging fish in that area.

An excellent way to keep lug-worms alive for several days is to place them, as you dig them, in a tin containing dry sand, but, even when actually fishing, see that the tin is not in the glare of the sun : a cool shady place is the ideal one. Of course, use a perforated cover so that air can enter the tin. When the lug-worm is freshly dug it is full of fluid, but, like lob-worms kept in damp moss, it improves and hardens with its exile in the dry sand.

While dealing with worms I should perhaps refer to the rag-worm. This creature is not very prepossessing in appearance, and resembles, in some respects, an elongated centipede. It is an excellent bait for grey mullet, and will also attract school bass and " flats," particularly on a sandy bottom. It can be found in the muddy banks of most estuaries. For digging it up a garden fork is the most efficient tool, as the mud is heavy, and rag-worms, in their natural environment, are not sluggish in their movements, hence a spade is not so satisfactory, especially as the mud conceals stones and pebbles.

The size of the rag-worms varies considerably, and the very small ones are not worth collecting. In selecting a spot on which to experiment, do not be tempted to try places that obviously have been well gardened : in angling phraseology they have been " over-fished." Search rather for fresh plots, such for example as that under an old mooring chain green with weed, there you may expect to find some of more mature age, some fat, lusty ones, a couple of inches long, something worth putting on your hook, and, *inter alia*, something to interest a roving fish. These rag-worms, if kept in a well ventilated tin, and in the shade, with a supply of the green weed that is peculiar to the estuaries, will serve you for a week or more.

Of the same species is the King rag ; thick, reddish objects, that are irresistible to most fish even when not on the feed. This type of worm is not so widely distributed as its lesser brother, and to obtain it you will need to get into touch with a seaside tackle shop that stocks it during the summer season.

We will now consider bait that, in one form or another, can, throughout the year, be seen in the fishmongers' shops. Of the different kinds, the mackerel is the most important. To make the best use of this fish it should be cut carefully, and each side will provide a number of excellent pieces.

46

Taking a sharp knife, and if possible using a board on which to place the mackerel, cut across the fish, about an inch and a half from the tail, then, as if filleting, run the knife along the backbone, towards the tail, but be sure to secure as much as you can of the tough skin terminating on the tail. When you have succeeded, you will have a piece of bait triangular in shape. This portion is called a " snead " in some districts, and a " last " or " laske " in others. It is the most valuable for your purpose. To employ it most advantageously, put the hook through the tough skin at the apex of the triangle, and push this hard skin over the eye of the hook, the shank of the hook should come along the middle of the fleshy side of the bait ; now push the barb right through the " snead." Next tie a bit of black cotton r o u n d the skin

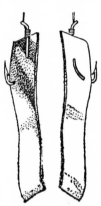

A secure method of hooking a mackerel " snead "

above the hook's eye, and you have a lure to be proud of. However rough the sea, the bait will flash around like a silvery fish ; and it will not be forced down into an uninviting lump in the bend of the hook. I have dealt with this item in detail, as I am a great believer in offering bait in the most attractive form. To proceed with the preparation of the remainder of the mackerel, cut across the fish, one side at a time, and obtain sections about three-quarters of an inch wide. Use these similarly to the tail bit, keeping the dark part at the top of the hook, so that the brighter part, with the barb in it, may scintillate in the moving waters. Having sliced the other side of the mackerel in a like manner, you will have enough bait for plenty of sport. One mackerel in the hands of an angler who can make a good job of the surgical operation will be more than equal to three fish hacked about by an inexpert person.

If mackerel are not in season, but you can buy a fresh herring, try that, treating it as you would a mackerel. Should your quest in that respect be unsuccessful do not despair, but fall back on a bloater or even a kipper, and prepare, as far as practicable, either of these alternatives as though you were going to employ a mackerel. Failing either of these expedients, do not hesitate, if yon see a heap of cockles in a fishmonger's shop, to try these as a means to the end, placing a sufficient number on the hook to cover it. Flat fish in particular are partial to this form of fare.

There are many other kinds of bait, but what is admirable for fishing from piers and similar places where you can let your tackle down gently will not stand up to a cast hurtling through a strong wind, and then taking a plop into a heaving sea. Perhaps, however, I should mention a few other baits in case you can procure them, and feel tempted to give them a trial. The chief of these are live prawn, mussel, spider crab and squid.

Many would-be beach anglers have told me that the difficulty in obtaining adequate bait has prevented them from taking up the sport. I admit that with a range of approved flies always at hand for salmon and trout, the question of lure for that class of angling is simplified ; while such bait as worms, gentles, paste, etc., presents no difficulties to the angler who enjoys coarse fishing ; still my experience has been that where there's a will there's a way, and the prospective sea angler need not be denied his fun, if he sets about his task in real earnest. Almost every day, during the whole of the year, I see the shore anglers busy with their rods, and that in itself is enough evidence to prove that some form of suitable bait is always at hand.

CHAPTER V

HOW TO FISH

THE heading of this chapter, "How to fish," may sound rather stupid, but there is far more in shore angling than meets the eye. Of course you can bait a hook, throw in—"throw in" mark you—and trust in providence. A writer once gave these tips as sure means of success when fishing from the beach. I am afraid that I am not in agreement with those views, and in fact, in my opinion, the advice does not promote angling, nor even fishing.

When I take my trout rod and set out on a dry-fly expedition, I wander along the river bank keeping a good look out for a rising fish, and then I try my luck. Similarly, when I accept the call of the seashore, I make up my mind to connect with a feeding fish. Though, of a certainty, I cannot in that sphere see direct evidence of what I hope to catch, yet my project then is to place my lure where I expect the fish to be. These words have been written as a prelude to the art of casting. To follow my meaning allow me to explain. Picture

Low water on a pebbly shore.

a fast river running into the sea : the tide is making, and where the fresh meets the salt, the boiling waters scour the bottom. Each side of the mouth a ridge of pebbles is piled high, mounting steeply almost from the bed that is composed of weedy stones and large boulders. A narrow belt of shingle, about two feet wide, separates the actual river bed from the pebbly ridge. As the tide gains, bass and other fish arrive from the deep water in search of a meal. Now the correct spot to place your bait is on the shingle. If you drop it amongst the stony obstructions in the middle of the surge, you will be courting a smash, while if you find the ridge, lead and bait will quickly become buried under the ever-shifting pebbles : hence you have to select a definite position, and cast out perhaps twenty yards.

Again in another part of the shore a weedy groin breaks the sweep of the sea, a glorious place to mark down your quarry. To put your tackle over the old piles would obviously be fatal, but you want to see your lead take the water not many feet away from the groin ; so to establish a perfect contact, you require to have complete control of your cast.

As another example, should the sea be rough, and you long for a big bass, your aim this time will be just beyond the roller that crashes and sends the foaming waters towards your feet : not a long cast for you to achieve, but one that must be accurate.

By now you will appreciate my point concerning the importance of casting.

No doubt, with practice, you will master the task but if you are a beginner, having had no opportunity of wielding any kind of rod, you will be well advised to serve your apprenticeship in a field before experimenting on the shore, and this for many reasons. To me there is nothing more annoying than for a fellow rodster to take up his stand near me, and put his line across mine. Accidents will occur I know, but there is a difference between a legitimate error of judgment and the irresponsible effort. The experienced angler has no difficulty in forming his opinion as to the cause of the blunder. A lead of four ounces on the end of a shooting line when out of control can inflict severe injury, and the risk is magnified out of all proportion should the beach be thickly populated by visitors. Further the novice can lose a deal of tackle if his mistakes in casting are many.

If you act on my suggestion, and repair to a field to try conclusions, merely assemble your rod and reel, and attach a lead of two ounces to your line. On another occasion you should ascertain the results when using a lead of four ounces. A good plan is to peg down pieces of paper, say fifteen, twenty, thirty and forty yards respectively distant from the spot on which you purpose standing. Let these marks denote the points of the compass North, South, East and West. You will thus be able to estimate the helping or resisting force of the wind, if any be blowing, while you will also accustom yourself to the angle of sunshine : both these factors enter into calculations when actually fishing.

In casting a fly on the river, you stand facing your objective, and employ an overhead whipping stroke, but shore casting, with a lead, is altogether a different problem : there you stand sideways, with one of your shoulders towards the place where you wish your lead to drop. Whether you cast in a right- or left-handed way appears to be a matter of choice. I have seen expert anglers attain success by each stance. Stand with your legs slightly apart, making sure that your feet are firm—remember that on the seashore you may be standing on pebbles that have an unhappy way of giving to your feet, just as you are making your cast—then unwind your line until you have the lead about four feet from the tip of the rod. Ready ? Now, with a free and an easy action, lob your lead out to the selected piece of paper, keeping your eye on the mark all the time. I use the word "lob," as I consider it most apt in this connection. There is no need to make a vicious gesture, the weight of the body and the turn of the wrist perform the deed without undue effort. You know what is meant by a "finished" batsman, you admire the "follow through" of the golfer, and you take pleasure in watching the stylist in any and every sport ; well, the next time that you are in the vicinity of anglers on the beach, scrutinize their casting methods, and you will understand my contention. As your line is travelling out, get into the habit of thumbing your reel. This is highly important, as your line must run smoothly, and above all must not over-run your reel. Should the latter error arise when fishing, you will stand the chance of a snap of your tackle, and probably, if not the whole trace, the lead at least will be lost. By thumbing your reel you will be ready to ease the pull of the weight when the desired spot has been reached, and you will thus not be vexed by a number of loose turns of line on your reel, which quickly occur if the reel is not checked in time.

After trying for half an hour, you will, no doubt, discover that you have mastered the game, and you will agree that the time has been well spent, for when you embark on actual business you will do so with every confidence, knowing the many snags to avoid ; snags that can spoil a day's pleasure, and ones that can incur unnecessary expense for you. Apart from all this, you will have the satisfaction of feeling that you are an asset to the guild. Further, to commence in the correct manner is as simple as starting on the wrong road, but to eradicate initial errors is a toil which is sometimes beyond the power of the average man.

Please do not run away with the impression that I am exaggerating the skill required in beach casting, as that is not my intention. I have laid special stress on the subject because I have met scores of anglers, even men who can throw a fly with precision, who seem incapable of grasping the idea, and I am saddened when I see a keen member of the craft committing a grievous fault over and over again.

When you begin the real attack from the shore, don't, when you have baited up and cast out, imagine that is the end of your labours, and place

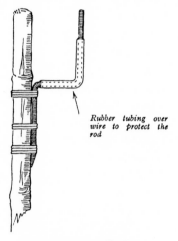

Rubber tubing over wire to protect the rod

A cheap and reliable rod rest can be made with a 4-foot bamboo and a piece of suitable wire as indicated above

your rod on a support. A support in the form of a forked stick, or other similar device, is useful at times when you want to attend to something else, but it is a snare.

Frequently you will notice a follower of the sport methodically rest his rod on an upright and fix a tiny bell to the tip of the rod. Personally I do not consider this angling, but regard it rather as killing time. True if a goodly fish accepts the bait, the bell will duly tinkle, but there is much more than this mere fact of which you need to be cognisant. There are such attractions as analysing the many kinds of bites, studying their peculiarities, and recognizing, as a corollary, what is paying attention to your lure. But in addition to the academic point of view, there is the material side which counts for a lot : therefore hold your rod, twist a turn of the line round your forefinger, and keep the line taut Now wait for consequences. If an artful flat fish comes along, quietly sucks in the bait, and lies still, you will know all about it, but the action was so gentle that a bell would not have been actuated. You, however, will strike, and hook that fish in the mouth : an easy one to unhook when you have it ashore. Had you relied on a bell, the fish would either have chewed through the gut and got away, or it would have worked the bait properly inside, and given you a surplus of bother to retrieve the hook. Possibly crabs will pester you, but you will be aware of their designs and, acting accordingly, you will not allow them to rob you of your bait : what is more you will not be in that unhappy

position of fishing with a denuded hook. I am
satisfied that the man who puts his rod on a rest
and trusts to luck loses more fish than he catches.

Now we come to the subject of "striking."
Experience counts for a great deal in deciding the
right second to strike. Though the following may
act as a rough guide, you will probably improve
upon it when, from time to time, you make contact
with your spoil, as the feel of a bite varies according
to the temperament of the angler.

A real lusty decisive bite should be accepted
immediately, and the strike should be firm and
sharp, sufficient to hook the fish, without being so
sharp as to risk a fracture of the tackle, for such a
bite usually denotes a good sized victim.

A drawing type of bite is customarily associated
with a flat-fish, and a few seconds should be allowed
for the feeding one to take the approved fare
completely into its mouth. After striking and you
receive no warning response, reel in a couple of
yards of line quickly, and pause. If you can detect
a movement, you have put your hook home. If
there is no sign of life, continue to wait, and be on
the *qui vive*, for the despoiled one will, most likely,
rediscover the delicacy, and deal with it in a more
energetic manner.

A bite that resembles a cheery "rap-tap" can
be regarded as the prerogative of a school bass : he
is a cheeky little fellow, and the "rap" is a
preliminary on the edge of the bait, his "tap" the

bait itself. Therefore if you encounter any bite of this description, do not strike at the " rap," but be ready to raise the top of your rod sharply in synchronism with the " tap." Many years ago I was greatly puzzled with this sort of bite. Again and again I struck, but obviously I was either too soon or too late, as I did not produce the fish, although when I reeled in I found that my bait had been partly torn from the hook. Feeling perplexed at the continual attacks without recording any success, I thought things out, and decided on a different plan of campaign : this time striking with the " tap." When I pulled in, I had a fighting little fury of about six ounces on my hook, and in half an hour afterwards, I accounted for four more. Now I am always ready for the rascals.

The final point after catching your fish, is how to land him. Anything up to a couple of pounds will not cause you any anxiety. All that you need do is to reel in steadily and speedily. As the weight mounts, however, the necessity for care increases in direct ratio. If you are into a big fish, and you sense trouble, a good idea is to walk backwards, meanwhile, keeping the line tight, and using your reel firmly. Should you be fortunate enough to form contact with a bass of, say, more than seven pounds, you will require all your wits to avoid a catastrophe : he may put up a fight that you pride yourself you can manage, but the test of your skill will come when you have coaxed him as far as the last large roller ; there beware, for then he will make his supreme endeavour to escape, and as the wave turns and breaks, he will plunge downwards with it. The resistance of the heavy crashing sea, combined with the power of a desperate fish, is enormous, and if there is a weak spot in your tackle, you will not be long in ascertaining where it is.

Another trick for which you want to be prepared, is that played sometimes by a large flat-fish. You are certain that you struck something hefty, but your line comes in slack : the reason is that the captive is swimming hard towards you, and meantime is trying to disgorge the bait. Walk rapidly up or down by the water's edge, at the same time reeling fast, with the object of tightening your line, and thereby curtailing the chances of your defeat.

Of course the story of a lost big one will add to your fishing repertoire, but I venture to suggest that your gratification will be greater on bagging a beauty, rather than in losing it : hence sound advice is to be always on the alert for any and every contingency as fishing is a queer game

CHAPTER VI

WHERE TO FISH

THE best place to select where to fish is, put in a nutshell, just where the fish are feeding. This may sound a trifle ambiguous, but if you are a devotee to the fly-rod, or you are an enthusiastic bottom angler, you will understand my meaning. In the same way as the salmon and sea-trout have their pools, and the coarse fish their particular haunts, so do the fish of the sea show definite predilections. The objective, therefore, of every shore rodster, should be to ascertain precise information concerning the habits of his quest. You may say that whereas the river is an open book, the sea, in its vastness, keeps its secrets. If you hold that opinion you are mistaken, as, believe me, it is quite as easy to read the sea as the river.

Nature whether of the air, the field, the river, or the sea, demonstrates the same inherent qualities. To live, all must feed ; and all by instinct know where to find their respective nourishments. Nature is ever ready to furnish us with a lesson. Even the insects can tell the tale. Everybody is

Where the river runs to the sea.

aware that where the flowers grow, bees and butter-
flies are to be found, but only the ardent gardener
can dilate on the various insect pests that await
the coming of his turnips, his broad beans, his
black-currants, his roses, and so on, and so on.
This fully versed gardener is thus a pattern for
the fishing zealot. It is passing strange, but everything in nature has something to thrive on it. The
fish of the fresh water, and the fish of the sea
provide a living for lice : nothing is immune to
attack, and nature decides that everything shall
have its fill. What is more remarkable, however,
is the fact that the means of obtaining the necessary
livelihood is handed down from generation to
generation. Hence, as we observe in the garden
and elsewhere, the denizens of the sea know what
they require, and, what is more, know where to
seek it. Our task, as shore anglers, is to ascertain
the needs and movements of our finny friends, then
to take advantage of the clues gleaned.

There was a time when I was quite content to
angle according to " the rule of thumb," but on
one summer's afternoon I was given cause for deep
thought. On the edge of a cliff, bordering a
delightful cove in Cornwall, I had stretched myself
for a laze. The heat was intense, the sea was
inert, and so fishing was out of the question.
Looking down on the clear bluish-green waters, I
could see the bottom easily, as the lovely silvery
sand seemed to reflect the sunbeams. To the left

and to the right of the inlet, dark masses of weedy rock made a striking contrast to the soft hued bed. Below me the lapping wavelets scarcely murmured, and the only sign of life was an inquisitive gull that settled on a lichen-covered stone not many yards away from me. The hot air made me feel drowsy, and I was not far removed from indulging in a siesta, when suddenly I noticed a large fish rounding the Western pile of rocks ; casually it nosed amongst the brown weed until it was joined by a similarly sized fish, then the pair moved straight across to the Eastern rocks. As the two passed I saw that they were pollock. Presently a few fish, which I decided were scad, followed the same route, and not long afterwards a couple of bass entertained me in a like manner. Now the mere fact of seeing the fish was not remarkable, but what did impress me was the deliberate passage, from rock to rock, of the various specimens without skirting the curve of the bay : they seemed as though they adhered to a charted course. Thinking that, perhaps, their action was due only to a coincidence, I made a point of visiting my place of outlook on three consecutive afternoons, and on each occasion I witnessed identical procedure on the part of other fish. No wonder, I thought, that not a thing had sampled my bait when angling from the beach of that cove, and I had tried conclusions down there for more than a week. The next evening found me on the Eastern side, where a cast could be made within a dozen yards of the rocks, and when the time came to pack up, two bass of about three pounds each in weight were waiting to be carried home.

Now, before wetting a line, I want to be satisfied that the bait will fall in the vicinity of hungry fish.

Broadly speaking, bass are sure to be met with round the mouths of estuaries, and for some distance up the tidal waters, as these fish are not over particular in their menu, and any garbage brought down by the fresh water is not likely to pass unheeded.

If you are acquainted with a place that provides deep water which flows strongly over rocks generously decorated with ribbon seaweed, you know the right spot to try for pollock.

If your project be to entice flat-fish, then you must rely on sandy bottoms.

Should you be a stranger to a seaside resort, where there are no local anglers from whom you can obtain the requisite tips, you will not go far wrong if you map out a systematic plan of espionage. First of all make a cursory inspection of the place, noting whether a river enters the sea in the neighbourhood, or if any rocky reefs break the waves, not forgetting to observe of what the shore is composed. Early acquaintance may convince you that good spots exist, but even so, you will be rewarded if you further probe the possibilities, while should your survey have failed to prove

63

interesting, the next step in your investigations should enable you to pick out the right position.

When the tide is low, wander along the cliff or high ground, and scrutinize the sea bed ; you will thus be able to ascertain, to reasonable and serviceable limits, where rocks exist, and particulars of the sandy stretches. If you notice a broad patch of sand with a reef of rocks on both sides, that solves your difficulty : mark it mentally. Perhaps you will remember it by a nearby clump of wind-swept trees, a mass of gorse, or a fall of cliff. Any object will serve, provided that you can detect it from the shore.

Next, saunter over the beach, and search for any outstanding characteristics. Probably you will discern a salient strewn with shells, remnants of crabs, and small masses of weed-covered mussels. This is an illuminating discovery. Obviously the sea currents are responsible for the collection, and just as patent is the deduction that, in this area, the fish are certain of a feed. This, then, is a likely bit of shore to try. Possibly it coincides with your mark on the cliff. If it does, you have been doubly successful. Should the cliff and beach marks not tally, then you have two distinct places from which to experiment.

Apart from the value of making these excursions, there is the added pleasure of feeling that you are stalking your game intelligently. Naturally if your efforts with the rod are not suitably recompensed after taking these precautions, you will, as a true angler, decide that the weather or the sea is unpropitious, and you will comfort yourself with the opinion that, on the next occasion, you will hook that specimen for which you are ever waiting.

Perhaps a river empties itself in the bay where you are spending your holidays. Now, there is a right and a wrong position to take up at the river's mouth. Assuming that the tidal conditions are suitable, be careful to place your bait where a fish will find it. The waves have commenced to pile up the river's flow, and the waters are boiling in their mighty conflict. Throw in a bit of stick, and watch its manœuvres : instead of it being swept out to sea, or forced up the river, it is tossed about for a time, and is eventually guided towards the water's edge. In a like manner any heavier matter brought down by the river is, after its buffeting in the turmoil, washed bankwards. You may not have given much consideration to this action, but the fish are not ignorant of the current's effect, and they search for their food where they expect to collect it. Do not, therefore, cast into the centre of the raging water, but immediately beyond it : your bait will thus fall in the place where the current would have carried a tit-bit naturally. If you are not actually fishing in the river's outfall, but in the sea by its side, do not cast into the track of the out-flowing fresh ; instead, take up your position about twenty yards distant from the mouth, as the currents outside act similarly to those inside. But here again, you need to take your bearings at dead low water. The storms and heavy seas of winter play havoc with the outfall: one time there will be a left turn, at another a right turn, and unless you see conditions when the tide is out, you, by relying on past experience, may be committing an unfortunate error. This variation in the waterway is more noticeable on a pebbly shore than on one of sand. The river bed that you recollect of last summer, when it presented simply a shingly strand, is now a deep one full of big rocks, as all the sand and shingle have been washed away. Last year you could cast there without compunction, this year you would find trouble. You cannot afford to take the run of a river for granted. What is more important, however, is that in some cases when the course of the river's outfall is in a certain direction, it offers an open way for incoming fish, whereas when it takes a different route, the high banks of pebbles and shingle which have been thrown up, cut off the track from the spawning grounds, and the bass, except during spring tides, have to travel round a reef of high rocks before reaching the river's mouth. Thus what during one season was an ideal piece of water, the following year the same water may prove worthless. The value of personal inspection, therefore, cannot be emphasized too much. With many other rodsters I share the view that the time spent in surveying prospective fishings, whether from the river bank or the seashore, is the most important aid to efficient angling. Naturally experience counts for a great deal in selecting the best point of vantage, when fishing in waters with which you are acquainted ; but in a fresh locality when you know for what to look, you will be surprised, having mastered the rudiments of the game, how quickly you can decide between the good and the indifferent stretches at your disposal. One thing of which you may be certain, if you act on this advice, is that you will not be numbered amongst those, and they are not a few, who use their sea rods where the waters are unprofitable.

There is a part of the coast, situated near a popular resort, which possesses its own peculiarities. About half a mile out is a deep channel course marked by buoys : between that channel and the water's edge the bottom is composed of flat weedless rock which one day is bare and another is covered by sand two or three inches in depth. In this particular area, well protected by a small headland, the tide rises and falls gently with, generally, scarcely a ripple. Obviously this is not the home of any crustacea ; and not a morsel of any kind is there to appease a marauding fish. On the rocky ledges of some near-by cliffs the cormorants build, and every day, out on the deep channel course, these voracious birds seek their prey, but they are too sage to waste their time on the barren waters closer to the shore ; the cormorant knows only too well the haunts of the fish. Yet year after year, during the holiday season, angling visitors may be seen along this stretch devoting hours to the impossible. Unfortunately these triers not only may form a wrong conception of shore angling, but they are likely to give the district an unfair reputation. To see these " hopefuls " for many a week failing to command success, simply owing to lack of foresight, is indeed a pathetic picture, and one that, no doubt, gives colour to that hoary joke of the " inmate " who said " Come inside."

CHAPTER VII

UNLIKE the rods for salmon and trout, and coarse fish, the sea-rod is never out of commission. Fresh-water anglers may, in their respective spheres, experience a poor season, then, on hanging up their rods, contemplate on the empty months that have to pass before they will sally forth again with renewed hope, but there is no close season for the sea angler ; all that he has to do is to pick out a fitting day, and be up and doing. If he strikes a poor patch, he is not bothered by the added trial of storing his rod for a few months ; he merely starts where he left off, and with determination to avenge the blank days.

Spring, summer, autumn and winter afford him plenty of opportunities to make a cast. Nor is he troubled to vary his fly, or change his bait, for the kind of lures that he uses in one season do service throughout the year, provided that they are obtainable.

Of the twelve months I scarcely know which one I prefer. Although sport may vary according to the conditions of the sea, yet I have sampled both good and bad days in each month of the year. True, winter brings cold blasts, but you know what

69

to expect, and you can take precautions accordingly. In summer, however, you do not prepare for an Arctic gust, and if you are caught in one you have cause to regret it. The seashore is subject to some strange extremes in temperature. On some days in March I have had to discard my coat, and in shirt sleeves seek comfort ; contrariwise, I have been perished with the cold on a July afternoon ; so of the various months the seasonal weather, as many may imagine, is not all-important.

For nine months of the year you may count on having the monopoly of the beach, and during that period you will not be disturbed by either bathers or paddle " floats," which are not altogether conducive to big bags. When the holiday season obtains, your chances of using the rod are somewhat diminished, especially if the sun works overtime, but even in August I have managed an hour's peaceful fishing, usually between one and two in the afternoon, when the water has been free of bathers. On the other hand, once in June I descended to a shore exceeding two miles in length : not a person could be seen, and I congratulated myself on the prospect of a quiet hour or so. Soon after my line was out, a party of about a dozen sauntered along the sands, stood beside me for a short while, and then, after undressing on the shore behind me, charged into the sea where my bait was resting. Their frolic over, they came in, and one of the male members remarked, " Sorry :

A QUIET SEA IN WINTER.

afraid we've spoilt your fishing." " Yes," I replied, adding " but I don't understand why you should have selected these particular few yards, with a mile vacant each side." His answer was very naïve : " Oh ! We thought that as you were fishing, the beach here would be sure to be safe for a dip."

One · more priceless gem. I was fishing from a beach that was deserted. Presently a man appeared accompanied by a black retriever. Reaching me he stopped, and after several minutes had elapsed, he threw a piece of wood into the sea for his dog to fetch : this procedure was repeated three or four times, although on each occasion, to regain the wood from the dog, the man had to stoop as he walked under my line. Finally glancing at me, he passed on, remarking, " Ah, I see you are fishing." Sometimes I am inclined to think that there must be some magnetic influence pervading anglers.

So much for the time of the year suitable—and unsuitable—for shore angling.

Now for the best time to fish. Undoubtedly when the tide is running in. I have compiled many records of my experiences with the sea-rod : date, weather, time of day, tide hour, and height of tide. The readings show that while I have caught fish at all stages of the flowing tide, my best achievements have been at approximately half tide, and this irrespective of all other elements. Hence whether sport has been poor or variable, enthusiasm grips me after the tide has been making for a couple of hours. Of course there is always the prospect of catching a fish when the tide is running out, if your position is at the mouth of an estuary where the fish move in and out with the tide, but the deterrent is that, with an ebbing tide, the water is continually receding from you, and you have to be constantly recasting.

The other elements to which I referred are many, and increase in proportion to your fastidiousness. After recounting them, you may be urged to ask whether there is a perfect day for shore angling. Well, you have, to a large extent, to rely on the weather, and though you may select a period that is fraught with fortuitous conditions, there is always the chance of something more promising.

When the wind whistles from the north-east, and the water takes on a clear and an icy appearance, there is small likelihood of attaining encouraging results.

A south-west breeze usually augurs well, as there is more balm in that air.

A little colour, produced by atoms of seaweed which has been thoroughly pulverized, can be placed on the credit side, but if a recent ground swell fills the water with masses of weed, your line will be continuously fouled. The only escape from this annoyance is to go in search of a section of the bay where the weed is not so prevalent. Frequently the currents will carry the debris in one direction, and you may be fortunate enough to discover a portion of the sea which is comparatively free.

A wind off the land is generally of poor avail, but when the tide is making, a gentle following breeze is ideal.

Weather that is designated as " quiet " can be regarded as good for flat fish, while the rougher the sea becomes so grow the possibilities of big bass.

You may wonder whether there is any magic in certain times of the day. Much has been written on this subject, but I must confess that I am not a convert to the fetish, although I am prepared to admit that at sundown the big bass are more likely to be hooked. As an old stager, I hold the opinion that if the fish are about you will catch them any day and any time.

In direct opposition to any hypothesis that there are correct and incorrect hours of the day, let me say that some of my most outstanding bags have come to hand on blazing hot afternoons in summer, when the sea has been flat and lifeless. While when conditions have been perfect, and I have anticipated some real sport, I have packed up without recording a bite. Mind you, I am referring to the same spot regarding these remarkable variations ; hence my advice is take your rod, and hope that the fish will be waiting for you.

Repeatedly I am asked if spring or neap tides offer the better facilities for shore angling. Experience has taught me that the question cannot be

73

answered dogmatically, as so much depends on other circumstances, and what may apply in one case is negatived in another.

I have the advantage of residing within three miles of a flat sandy bay, a steep pebbly shore, an estuary, and a river's mouth. As the spirit moves me I try each, and consequently I recognize no hard and fast virtue in a spring tide. On a sandy beach this tide undoubtedly serves a useful purpose because, by running up much farther, it disturbs and washes out a not inconsiderable quantity of mutilated crustacea and other refuse dear to the roving bass and flat fish. The only drawback, if you regard it as such, is that, with the waves encroaching rapidly, you have to be continually moving your impedimenta up the sands.

On a pebbly shore there is little garbage for a high tide to absorb, and here the water simply registers a greater depth ; not that you fish in much deeper water, because you are forced back to a higher ridge of pebbles.

Considering the estuary, the balance there is more even, and what you gain in one way you lose in another. With a neap tide you can cast much nearer the deep water channel where the fish move, but the spring tide supplies an opportunity for the waves to scavenge the upper shores. The latter tide, however, flows past you more strongly, and in addition to the need of a heavier weight, casting must be performed with greater frequency than with a slack tide.

A general agreement cannot be reached concerning the benefits or otherwise of a spring tide operating at the river's mouth. Unquestionably the bigger volume of water there attracts more fish, but after the salt has conquered the fresh, the rush of the former is so powerful that difficulty arises in finding a safe anchorage for the lead, while each tide at this period tears away such a harvest of green weed which is common to the lower reaches of the river's banks, that in no time your line is so decorated that it resembles a curry-comb. This collection acts as an abnormal resistance to the racing current, and valuable time is wasted in reeling in, clearing the encumbrance, and re-casting. By now, no doubt, you appreciate the danger of plumping whole-heartedly for a spring tide.

Another " nut " that is often passed to me, during my peregrinations on the seashore, is whether better returns are forthcoming when the sky is overcast or clear. The old-fashioned fallacy that fishing can be undertaken on only cloudy days still persists, and sometimes I wonder when this, which nearly amounts to a superstition, will die. There are many such quaint ideas connected with angling, and from the many rodsters whom I meet, expert and amateurs, I come across all kinds of nonsense. One really fervid disciple of the sea-rod once assured me that flat fish would not bite if the sun was obscured, and he actually believed in this doctrine. I am afraid that these fables do not appeal to me.

75

I recollect some years ago staying at a popular riverside resort where the killing of trout was the chief object. After lunch on one hot cloudless day in late August all the rods were resting, as the general opinion was that nothing could be accomplished on the river until late in the evening. Although I agreed in the main, I had made up my mind to carry out a special stratagem with a bonny fish that I knew favoured a certain pool not far up the river. This particular bit of water was difficult to negotiate, as the far side, deep and black, skirted a perpendicular cliff some twelve feet high, the bottom of which gave root to a few bushes and weeds. To cast from that side was out of the question ; even dapping was impracticable owing to the far-reaching undergrowth, besides this desirable trout spent his leisure away back in the shade of the bushes. The near bank rose about three feet above the water which could not be waded, while, apart from one small hawthorn bush, there was no cover. I had given the fish, the banks, and the means of access to the pool much deliberation. The prospects were certainly not promising, but I resolved to make a supreme effort. Stealthily approaching the hawthorn bush, which seemed to become smaller and smaller as I neared it, I studied the scene again and made calculations. At the head of the pool, standing out from the tangled growth on the opposite side, was a cow-parsnip with some very fine leaves. My objective was to place my fly on the leaf nearest the water. The risk was immense, as an awkward blackberry bramble drooped across the spreading plant. To cast a few inches too far would entail a smash, and a short cast would defeat my intentions. Taking extra care I whipped my fly across, and when I saw it alight on the selected leaf, a thrill went through me ; my luck was in. So far so good : reeling up steadily, my line was soon straight, and ready for the next move. At such a time much could be lost by over-impatience, hence I waited some seconds, then gently raised the tip of my rod. The fly gradually travelled over the leaf, and fell naturally on the water. At the same instant the well-known ring told the tale. When my victim came to the net, I realized that it was the best trout that had ever fallen to my artifices, and on returning to my hotel, the capture was the topic of conversation for many an hour. I mention this incident in no spirit of vainglory, but only as an illustration of the mistake in attaching too much importance to climatic conditions.

My advice, therefore, is fish whenever the opportunity presents itself, and don't be influenced unduly by all the varying opinions that you hear regarding the weather.

To nothing so much as to angling does that well-worn adage apply : " If at first you don't succeed, try, try, try again."

CHAPTER VIII

WHEN TO USE FLOAT TACKLE

ALTHOUGH somewhat outside the scope of shore fishing as it is usually accepted, a sinker being the customary method, this book would be incomplete without a reference to the resort to float tackle.

If a heavy sea is running, with big waves pounding the beach, bringing with them a mixture of all kinds of weed, to keep a lead well out is almost an impossibility, while a bite would probably go unnoticed amongst the incessant jars caused by ribbon weed attached to stones constantly fouling the line. At such a time fishing with ordinary weighted tackle is calculated to fray the temper of even the most patient angler, for no sooner is the cast completed, and the line reeled taut, than the strong current and the floating debris bring in the bait. But this is the right moment to change over to float tackle, as now the really big bass are on the prowl, seeking those choice treasures which the tumbling waves stir out of the sands.

Resource should be made, if possible, to stouter tackle ; line and trace of a greater breaking strain, and a larger hook, for should a bass favour your bait, you may be certain that your catch in this boisterous sea will, on the law of averages, be something heavier than five pounds ; more likely a fish of eight or ten pounds in weight will have to be coaxed ashore ; and not merely with a fighting fish will you have to contend, but with the enormous pull of the waves aided by any weed your float, swivel and leads have appropriated.

In describing the assemblage of the tackle, perhaps I had better refer to the float in the first place. The ordinary sea floats are unsuitable for this kind of rough work, as you will not be able to depend on sight for your bites : feel is the only true signal under these conditions. A tip given to me many years ago by an angler who had been accustomed to fish in foreign as well as in British

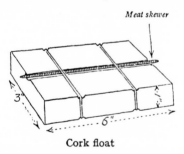

Cork float

waters, has stood me in good stead many times in each year since. His recipe was, after finding a piece of discarded cork from a lobster pot, cut it into a rectangular shape, about six inches in length,

79

and from three to four inches wide : the usual
thickness of these corks is an inch. Make in the
middle a small hollow lengthways, sufficient in
depth to carry a wooden meat-skewer ; the skewer
to extend half an inch at each end of the cork.
Nicking the cork about an inch from both ends, tie
a piece of line tightly round the cork where you
have made the notches. Now when you push the
skewer along the groove, it will be firmly held.

This float fulfils a dual purpose, not only does it
keep your line afloat, but it acts as a weight to take
out your line, and you will be surprised at the
casting power of this piece of cork, especially when
it is sodden.

This float is so fashioned that it can easily be
brought into use. All that you have to do, after
removing the skewer, is to thread your line along
the groove, under the ties, then replace the skewer.

The trace, either of gut or gut substitute, should
be three feet in length. At one end attach the
hook, and at the other end provide a swivel, in
this instance you will find one measuring one-and-
a-half inches most serviceable.

Some three inches away from the swivel fit a
spiral lead, one of two inches ; also, about one foot
six inches from the hook, fit another spiral lead of
similar size. The objects of these leads, placed at
the distances indicated, are for the top one to take
the cast down immediately into the water, and for
the lower one to curb the action of the bait.

Remember, I am suggesting tackle for a truly heavy sea : should the sea moderate you may dispense with the lower lead.

Before actually putting the tackle into use, a good plan is to test, at home, the weights against the carrying capacity of the float : simply tie the

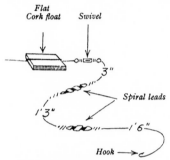

Float and trace for big bass

swivel to the cork, coil the trace and leads, loosely tying the coil to keep it together, and drop the lot into a bucket of water. If the float cocks, the leads are too heavy, but if the float remains flat your gear is just right.

To assemble your tackle, mount your float at the extreme end of the line, then attach the cast. You will notice that your float, coming next to the swivel, cannot slip down the trace ; further, and this is equally important, the float acts as a guide to the length free for casting. Merely reel up until the float is within six inches from the top of the rod, and you have the ideal amount of slack to make a perfect cast.

The bait suitable for this class of fishing is a " snead " or strip of mackerel, or of one of its alternatives referred to in the chapter headed " Bait " ; the idea being to suggest a small silvery fish flashing about in the rising and falling waters.

Now, where to place your lure. There is no necessity to make a long cast, as the bass are close in when you are trying with this tackle. Looking out to sea you observe the waves come sweeping in until finally the last one crashes not far from you, Behind this mighty roller is where you must drop your bait, not too close to the climbing wave or the float will be washed in, but just far enough away, so that the undertow can neutralize the flowing water. If your first attempt at this mark is not successful, do not hesitate to reel in and cast again, for anywhere but in the right spot is courting failure in your efforts to account for that specimen.

This type of tackle, but of a lighter description, can be employed with every prospect of good results on calmer days, if you can find a suitable position on a rocky ledge jutting out from the shore and where, by casting out either to the left or right of the point, the current will carry your float away from you. Any of the baits previously mentioned may be used for this kind of angling. One spiral lead, however, will prove adequate, and it should be attached about half-way down the

An estuary that the school bass haunt.

cast. One advantage of fishing from such a ledge, and in this way, is that whether the tide is making or receding matters naught, as on an incoming tide you cast from one side, and on the ebbing tide you try from the other side of the rocks.

Perhaps an estuary empties itself near where you are staying, in which case, should the school bass be present, you are safe for plenty of fun, especially if you are a roach enthusiast. Of course much depends on the character of the estuary. Some estuaries drain right away, leaving merely a central fast running water-course, with muddy sides. In others, at low tide, the remaining water branches out, forming stagnated pools. The latter kind of estuary provides the best opportunity for the " lipper," as the roach angler is designated in some districts ; for the small bass in goodly sized shoals frequent these quiet pools. A light rod, and tackle designed for roach fishing are required. The best bait is the small rag-worm. Casting into one of these pools, the angler has not long to wait for the tell-tale jerk of his float. A quick strike, and business has begun. On such occasions it is not unusual for a dozen or a score of fish averaging about four to the pound, to be the sequel to an hour's work. The right time to experiment is approximately an hour after dead low water, that is when all the tidal water has ebbed, and the pools have settled down.

Naturally you will want to know your estuary

thoroughly, particularly if you have to adopt wading measures, as there is scarcely a more treacherous bottom than that which is to be found there.

If the estuary boasts a jetty or a bridge, then when the tide is sufficiently high, you can essay your heavy float tackle, especially when the light is fading, in the hope of connecting with an outsize bass.

As the surface of the water here is comparatively smooth, and casting is little more than dropping your bait into the swiftly moving current, you can dispense with your home-made float, and use one of the pattern known as the " Fishing Gazette " : an excellent float in all respects, and one that can easily be attached to your line.   You will appreciate this great advantage if you are fishing when darkness is falling, and you decide to change to a larger float, for the exchange can be accomplished in a matter of seconds.   When fishing in a bad light a float with a white top is preferable, as its progress with the stream is more discernible.

One satisfactory feature in fishing from a jetty or a bridge is that you can play out your line until your float carries your bait to the exact position where you have reason to believe a bass will be feeding, and another happy phase is that you can enjoy your sport equally well on a flowing or an ebbing tide.   Further, there are ideal spots both above and below the structure from which you are fishing. The local anglers are fully alive to them, and if you

are lucky enough to be able to watch a resident
expert, you will see that he will manœuvre his float
until it comes to rest in the vicinity of the outfall
of a small drain : knowing what the bass is seeking,
he will do his best to satisfy the hungry fish. The
most fitting bait to use in this instance is either
soft or " peeler " crab.

Before finishing with this interesting method of
angling, and the very important part that it plays
in dealing with the fish that visit these estuarian
waters, mention must be made of that shy fish, the
grey mullet. Probably there is no more tantalizing
sight than to see hundreds and hundreds of these
fish, in vast shoals, calmly swimming round and
round, utterly indifferent to the well-baited hooks
that bar their passage. Again and again, at the
mouth of an estuary, I have seen a dozen or more
rods ready to radiate the glad message which
rarely materialized, and down in the murky waters
a mass of grey mullet performing all manner of
weird tactics. I can plead guilty to the lack of
ability to circumvent these rogues. Many days
following my hopes have been raised, but although
I have tried every kind of wile, the net results of
my efforts have never exceeded two fish at any
one time, yet my lure has been in the midst of what
seemed a multitude of grey mullet so thick that,
as shoal after shoal advanced, wheeled, and
retreated, my float has quivered with the bumping
and boring against the line.

Strange as it may seem, the only occasions on which my bait has been accepted has coincided with catches by the other rodsters alongside of me, and ten minutes have proved long enough for these fish to obtain their fill, as far as our contributions were concerned. Thus the angler who landed his quarry, baited up again slickly, and cast out immediately, usually added a second mullet to his bag, but no more. After that short spell of good fortune we had to be content to witness the same mass formation and gyrations of these remarkable fish.

Our success was always attained when the water was at its lowest level, and we decided that the solution of the mystery was to be found in the state of the water. Grey mullet are notoriously partial to estuaries and harbours where the taint of sewage exists, hence at low tide the " seasoning " would be more piquant.

Of the many varieties of baits employed none equalled the killing qualities of the small ragworm used in conjunction with exceedingly light tackle.

That there is nothing new in the quaint rovings of these thickly packed mullet shoals in our estuaries, is borne out by the stories told by the " old hands " who remember, in the dim past, the days when " they used to go snatching," as they say. " That is the way to be certain of gathering a good harvest," they will tell you, " snatching." The method these old poachers adopted, was to

86

cast out a weighted line, carrying some treble hooks, and pull the contraption rapidly through the shoal, with the consequence some of the fish were foulhooked. To listen to these tales is very illuminating, but glad we are, and future generations will be that such practices were made illegal, otherwise, for us and those to follow, sport, poor as it is with grey mullet to-day, would be a much more sorry affair.

CHAPTER IX

ODDS AND ENDS

SO much has been written about what would-be anglers are supposed not to know, and so little concerning what is taken as granted they do know, that to enlarge on the latter phase will not be out of place, especially as there is always a danger in assuming that that which is regarded as obvious is too insignificant to dwell on.

As an example of elementary detail which is so often neglected, but which more than repays for a little attention, is the care of the tackle. To form good habits in this respect may entail a small expenditure of minutes, but bad habits will prove a spendthrift of hours ; besides, there is a joy to be gained by the possession of well-kept gear, apart from the satisfaction of knowing that, as far as you are responsible, your tackle will not fail you.

First of all, consider your rod. Do not put it away leaning against a wall, for it to become warped, but hang it up by the loop provided at the top end of the bag. Then not only will it keep straight and true, but it is out of everybody's way. Occasionally give the rod a rub with an oily rag, particularly the metal parts and reel fitting, seeing that the latter functions smoothly ; keep the rings free from sand. Do not forget that salt water and sand quickly breed a variety of troubles. If the windings show signs of ravelling, use a little " Durofix," or other similar remedy immediately ; a spot in time will save ultimate professional repairs.

Next give periodical attention to your reel which should be taken to pieces, cleaned and oiled. Of course, if you allow sand to accumulate inside, do not blame the reel or something else, if, when casting, the reel stops revolving, and your lead breaks away at a tangent. How often have I witnessed this contretemps ; how often have I heard the reel abused in no uncertain manner, and to think that a few minutes devoted to this important article would have obviated all those unpleasantries.

Now we come to the line : every time after fishing do not fail to wash out the salt water. Simply transfer the line to an ordinary wood winder, or a piece of wood as an alternative, immerse in fresh water for several minutes, and finish off with

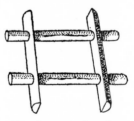

Wooden winder for washing line. If the line is wound alternately from side to side and top to bottom the salt water can be eliminated quite easily

two or three washings in more fresh water. I usually

89

drop my line into water in the scullery sink, let it soak there, and then hold it under running tap water for some seconds. Shake as much water out of the line as possible, then hang up the line either out in the fresh air, or somewhere inside the house, and reel it up when thoroughly dry. You may be inclined to think that you can dispense with this programme. If so, try fishing on two or three consecutive days, and see what you can do with a water-logged line. You will not be in doubt afterwards as to the efficacy of a dry line. In addition to the immediate value of caring for your line, there is the subsequent benefit. If you put away your line every time after use without cleansing it, the day is not far distant when, having hooked a fair sized fish that puts up a bit of a fight, you will suddenly discover that from the tip of your rod you are waving a few yards of slack line, and to your chagrin, you will find that your line is rotten.

Probably you will decide that the trace, hooks, swivel and lead cannot go wrong. If so you will be mistaken. I have tried a number of rust-proof hooks suitable for salt water, but whether the salt water, the bait, or the combination of the two is responsible I know not, but I do know that these hooks speedily deteriorate if not washed in fresh water and dried. Even the gut, where tied to the brass swivels and to the brass loop of the lead respectively, soon develops an ominous black mark if left without attention, and a sudden jerk causes a fracture. Therefore wash in fresh water this portion of your tackle, dry thoroughly, clean away any remnants of bait attaching to the hooks, and satisfy yourself that the points of the hooks are sharp. Often when reeling in, your hook fouls a stone, and the point is damaged. A small file will overcome this defect.

You may consider that these little tasks constitute unnecessary fuss. Well, I am prepared to agree that everything is a matter of opinion, but the advice is offered to you in the light of experience. I bought mine, and at times paid a long price for it, as there is nothing more galling than to lose a good fish through sheer negligence in looking after the tackle. Hence these heart to heart tips are no more and no less than " tricks of the trade."

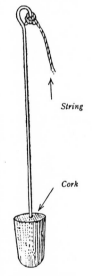

String

Cork

Disgorger. The string and cork are important

While on the topic of tackle, there is one small implement that calls for notice, namely the disgorger. Should you need this instrument, you will want it to hand at once. Unfortunately it can be elusive, and lay hidden amongst other gear in the bag ; therefore to guard against this annoyance, an excellent plan is to keep a large cork on the pointed end, and with a piece of string through the eye at the other end, have it tied to a button or tab in the fishing bag.

Not infrequently my opinion is sought by budding shore anglers regarding the virtue or otherwise of rubber boots. Speaking in general terms, these boots are indispensable during seven months in the year, especially if you wish to cross the mouth of a river, or where the beach is unduly flat. Angling from pebble ridges, however, the need is not so apparent. Of the different patterns procurable, thigh boots are the best. Waves have an eerie knack of rushing in with considerable force every now and again, and the water then runs insidiously up the shiny surface of the rubber, hence an ordinary knee boot is a snare. Even with thigh boots, tied at the top, I have been caught napping ; and when the trapped water has found its level, the result is anything but comfortable. These boots are rather heavy and tiring if worn for a long period by anyone not accustomed to them, but drawbacks can be levied against most things. When about to wear sea-boots a good plan is to first pull on a pair of sea-boot stockings which are made of a coarse and hard natural wool : this natural wool is full of oil, and the stockings are supposed to be waterproof.

After using rubber boots, give them a dip in fresh water, with the object of removing the salt which has been left on them by the sea-water.

Do not forget to give rubber boots an airing if they have not been worn for some time : hang

FLAT SANDS AND TALL CLIFFS.

them upside down, with a stick inside the top to keep that part open.

During the five warmer months, resource may be made to shorts, or turned-up slacks, providing that you wear sand-shoes, as a precaution against broken glass and rusty tins that seem to possess special designs on bare feet. If you paddle about in this manner by the hour do not forget, before you start, to rub a small quantity of olive oil into your skin, otherwise the action of the sea-water, plus that of the sun, will cause you to remember the trip days afterwards, for on retiring to bed, following the day out, you will find that your legs are swollen, and that they resemble earthenware drain pipes in shape and hardness.

Possibly you will decide on a comfortable time, and seek the aid of a folding seat. This is suitable on a sandy shore, though with a flowing tide you will be on the move continuously. Eventually when you have to retreat to shelving shingle or pebbles, your seat will be more trouble than it is worth. For that position you cannot improve on a folded old overcoat or a ground-sheet. You may smile at the suggestion of a ground-sheet : if so, the next time that you are on the sands, so warm and dry in the blazing sun of summer, scoop out an inch or two of this lovely sparkling surface, and you will come to dark, damp undersand. Not the result of sea-water, mark you, but evidence of fresh water draining from the high land. I often marvel when I see the summer visitors, so careful not to sit on damp earth, spending hours reclining on sand that ofttimes a couple of inches down is little more than a stream. One day, speaking on the subject to a medical friend, he replied, " Ah, you don't see the consequences, either immediate or ultimate." That is so ; these visitors are enjoying themselves to-day, but to-morrow they will be home once more, with probably a packet of unknown trials.

Whilst on the matter of comfort, do not forget that on the seashore the wind can be most treacherous. During the bleak months a waistcoat or coat of leather is a great asset ; further if a strong sea is running, some protection against the drifting fine spray should be provided. You may not notice this driving mist, but take a peep either side of you, and you will see what appears to be a grey cloud rolling in. After all, there is much to be said for making your expedition one of pleasure and, at the same time, guarding against minor and major ailments.

If at first you do not feel inclined to take up shore fishing in earnest, but merely want to toy with the idea for an odd week by the sea, without incurring much expense, you can always fall back on a mounted sea line : this, made up of some thirty yards of line, with lead and two hooks on gut, together with a hard wood winder, can usually be purchased for a couple of shillings. After a trial with this contrivance you may be tempted to embark on something more professional. Although I recollect some years ago seeing a dear old couple perfectly content to fish with their hand lines from the shore. Day after day, when the weather was kind, and the tide served, these two would arrive with their seats. The old gentleman, no amateur in beach lore, was adept at swinging the lead, and he would put both the lines far out ; then he and his wife, holding taut lines, would settle down to await the advent of cheery tokens. When either secured a prize he never failed to wave his hand in jubilation to me, and these two did surprisingly well, often comparing satisfactorily with specialists using rods.

As a final tip, if you are " smitten " with the sport, do not hesitate to take in an angling paper or magazine. Not only will you pick up some valuable information from these publications, but you will be interested to read what the other fellow is doing ; and when you learn that, somewhere or other, a " specimen " has been landed, you will be overjoyed to think that there are just as good fish in the sea as ever came out.

CHAPTER X

PRAWNS

IN chapter four, under the heading of " Bait," mention was made of a variety of useful lures ; and of many of these necessities, details were given concerning how, when and where they could be obtained, together with advice regarding the best methods of storing them, but possibly you noticed that prawns, a most deadly artifice, were dismissed without more than a passing reference. There was a reason for the omission of specific particulars in connexion with these delectable delicacies, for as such they deserve a few chapters to themselves, particularly as to allude to " prawning " is to open up an entirely new sport peculiar to the seashore, a sport that is both fascinating and, from a " table " aspect, most remunerative.

Prawns may be placed in the luxury class of comestibles, and to buy are certainly in the expensive region. In the latter category I do not refer to the imported tinned ones, but to " English large " as they are quoted in the Billingsgate wholesale price list. During the season you will see them

A SANCTUARY FOR PRAWNS AND LOBSTERS.

marked, according to the month, at anything ranging from four shillings to ten shillings a pound, and when you purchase them at a retail figure, you will be asked twopence, threepence, or even fourpence apiece. Hence if you go " prawning " and bring home a hundred, fifty, or merely a score, your return will, I venture to think, be welcomed. Naturally I am referring to big prawns, in size when cooked that, from the tip of the whisker to the end of the tail, will measure some eight inches. " Grandfathers " we used to call them along the south-west coast, and, strange as it may seem, I have heard them spoken of in like manner on the Pembrokeshire shore.

Should you be an angler you will return any immature fish that you hook, so, if you decide to test your fortune with a prawning net, do not retain the small fry, but give them a chance to wax large and luscious. I mention the point at this stage, as on many occasions I have seen visitors bagging hundreds and hundreds of tiny creatures that, when taken from the saucepan, can amount to only heads and tails. I am fully alive to the fact that these regrettable depredations are due entirely to ignorance on the part of the enthusiasts, and I trust that these words of warning will reach some receptive minds.

Not long ago I was waiting to be served in a fishmonger's shop, and each time that the proprietor passed a dish of freshly caught, freshly cooked prawns he helped himself to one. Laughingly he remarked to me, " If I don't sell this lot soon I shall devour them," adding " The one thing I can't resist is a prawn." Perhaps, should you set out on a prawning venture in the pursuit of a few for bait, you may, if very successful, alter your decision and have them cooked. That will probably be your undoing, and henceforth you will not use them for the original purpose, but for your personal enjoyment, thereby following somewhat the example of the fishmonger. Personally I hesitate to employ these toothsome dainties for bait when I can obtain something less savoury.

For me a spell of a couple of hours with the net offers as much fun as a similar time with the rod, as the same spirit of adventure is awakened. Once more the game is one of scheming to encompass the victim, once more the game is a battle of wits, and once more, as the chances are not wholly unequal, the encounter enters the realm of sport.

As with shore angling, there are several factors to be considered, such as the necessary implement to use, how to prawn, where to prawn, and when to prawn : these are equally important for the achievement of success, and each item deserves careful and methodical study. Of course you can wander out, net in hand, and take " pot-luck," but, like all other sporting efforts, there is much more in the pastime than just that.

I have an acquaintance who, throughout the

summer, makes a point of trying every suitable
tide. He is on the aged side, and
does not hurry himself, but while
other more energetic prawners are
dashing from pool to pool, and
complaining of small returns, the
one of age and experience quietly
plods along, often tackling pools
which have been spoken of as
being quite hopeless, and at the
end of the trip he can usually
show a basket of a hundred or
more real beauties, together with
a lobster or two, whereas each
of the more impetuous netters
can display scarcely more than
a score as a result of his labours.
Many times when operating I
have stopped to have a word with
this " professional," and generally
he has remarked, " They say there
is nothing in this pool, wait a
minute and I'll show you." Then,
almost casually, he has worked his
net towards a selected spot, and
on its withdrawal, announced,
" Told you as much, three
' Granfers.' " You may be sure I

Live prawns
mounted in
tandem

have profited by these lessons, and his cheery
advice, so in the course of the following chapters

99

I will endeavour to impart the knowledge which I have gained from my master.

I should perhaps emphasize the fact that I am dealing with shore prawning, in other words prospecting in the numerous pools left by the ebbing tide

CHAPTER XI

PRAWNING GEAR

THE gear required is both simple and inexpensive, but the actual cost is not so important as is the selection of the right type of net. All kinds of nets are displayed in the shops at seaside resorts ; large, small and medium, some with wooden frames, others with hoops of iron, many round in shape, and not a few fashioned in fantastic forms. Of the numerous patterns for your choice, there are ones that are totally unsuitable, others that may be described as makeshifts, and in a lesser number some that will pass without unfavourable criticism. I have experimented with most makes, sometimes owing to spending a holiday in a fresh spot by the sea, and not having armed myself with my trusted friend.

The net that has proved itself pre-eminent in my hands for many years, and the one that I can thoroughly recommend is formed of a flat iron hoop, of ten inches in diameter. The hoop is provided with holes at intervals of an inch, and through these holes a stout copper wire is threaded. To the wire is attached an ordinary corded net. To appreciate the reasons for these specifications, you must remember that where you are going to prawn

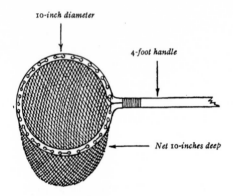

10-inch diameter

4-foot handle

Net 10-inches deep

Prawning net

The net is attached to the rim with copper wire which is passed through the holes as indicated above

the rocks are ragged and sharp ; therefore if the net is not protected where it is attached to the frame, breakages will quickly appear. Further, not infrequently, the frame becomes wedged between the rocks, and a little rough handling is not conducive to fair wear and tear. Copper wire is more impervious to the action of the salt water than is the ordinary cheaper kind. The size, of ten inches in diameter, is admirable for probing all likely places ; a larger circumference will probably be too unwieldy for your purpose. The handle which should be about four feet in length, must be strong and securely fitted to the frame. The only snag that I have noticed with these nets, and which, by the way, is common to most patterns, is that the net is not deep enough, and the prawn is given an opportunity of hopping out before it is grasped and placed in confinement. Perhaps to state here would not be inopportune that, when the actual net wears out, a " spare part " can be purchased. So to overcome the difficulty of a shallow net I usually cut along the bottom of the original net and introduce, by neat tacking, the supplementary one. By this means I am provided with a net of about ten inches in depth which gives me entire satisfaction.

Before leaving the subject of the net, I shall do well in reminding you to wash the net and the iron hoop thoroughly in fresh water after use, while when the net is stored for the winter, do not forget to grease the iron parts, otherwise rust will soon take its toll.

The only other essential that you will need to take with you, is something in which to carry your spoil. As the prawns must be kept alive until, for cooking purposes, they are dropped into boiling water, a basket or some similar contrivance will be most suitable. The old-fashioned creel, so beloved by anglers a few decades ago, can be pressed into this duty with every advantage. If you are not a proud possessor of this utility, you can fall back on a home-made bag, composed of linen crash which is exceedingly strong though porous, or failing that ordinary canvas, measuring twelve inches in width and fifteen inches in depth. A good idea is to provide yourself with two such bags, or a creel and a bag, for should you entice a lobster into your net, you will need a carrier in which to restrict its activities.

One more tip, and that is do not forget to see that you are not minus your pocket-knife, also take with you a supply of string, or better still some fishing line, for, however careful you may be, sooner or later a sharp edge of rock will cut your net where it is connected to the frame. An immediate repair will save you much annoyance at the time, together with more extensive mending subsequently. That we should neglect such obvious precautions seems very strange, but on many occasions I have been approached by unhappy prawners, with the request for a bit of string or the loan of a knife.

As I mentioned " cooking purposes " in this chapter, perhaps I ought to state here that, if you are in doubt concerning the way in which prawns should be cooked, all you require is a saucepan of boiling water, to which some salt has been added. Drop the prawns into the saucepan—they meet with a sudden death—and keep the water boiling gently for some eight minutes. Dish up and let them cool.

CHAPTER XII

HOW TO PRAWN

THIS simple heading of " how to prawn " may create the impression that there is some knack in the use of the net, so I will state at once that the sport is not so easy as it appears to be. To assist you in making the most of your endeavours, a few words concerning the haunts and habits of the prawn may be helpful.

As the sea recedes you will notice that each of the pools left behind apparently does not vary much in depth. True, the general depth of one may average a foot, another three or four inches, but as the tide ebbs these pools will gradually drain away. The prawns have sufficient instinct, however, to avoid the ones which will eventually lose all their water, and will take refuge in those where some water will remain. The prawns are aware of the spot where the residue, usually under a weedy rock, will give them shelter, and there they will collect until the tide turns. Further, they also select pools edged with rocks under which ledges run back one, two, or more feet : there they have sanctuary from the ever watchful gull.

The ideal moment to put your net to good purpose is when the pools have " settled down," as we locals describe them, then the prawns have congregated for their rest. Of course those perfect conditions are only possible when you have the prawning grounds at your sole disposal. If you are one of many seekers of the prey, you cannot afford to wait, and you must be satisfied with the best of the available opportunities. Should you be conversant with the lie of the shore, you will have little difficulty in selecting the most promising spots. A stranger, however, is thrown on his own resources, but he will not take long in summing up the situation sufficiently so as to enable him to make a wise choice.

Having marked down a desirable pool, do not commit the mistake of being in too great a hurry, but push your net quietly under the ledge of rock, moving it along almost on the bed of the pool. Satisfy yourself that your net has reached the extreme end of the cavity, then raise it until you feel you are in contact with the roof of the opening : withdraw the net somewhat rapidly, and if a prawn was in hiding, you may be certain to have accounted for it. Perhaps you have drawn blank ; in that case do not despair, but work, in a similar manner, under all the rocks surrounding that pool. Should a boulder occupy a position in the pool, do not fail to search that, as well as the bordering ledges, for the prawns do not always frequent the same cracks. The direction of the wind and the set of the tide account for the different harbourages which the creatures will affect on two days running : but there is method in the seeming madness of these prawns. Suppose that there is an easterly wind of sufficient force to move the breaking waves slightly with it ; on such an occasion if you study a pool into which the tide is flowing you will notice that the water on the western side is very disturbed owing to the wavelets running against the rocky edge, whereas on the opposite side the steady flow produces little effect. In those circumstances you may be assured that the visiting prawns will select the quiet side, as they would enjoy little leisure with the chopping waters.

If your initial pool, therefore, proves valueless, take heart, for probably, when the tide was flowing, the pounding waves acted as deterrents to a pleasant entry.

On many occasions I have netted the grounds when, much to my surprise, one good pool after another has yielded nothing, then in the next pool, not usually regarded as a sound proposition, I have scooped out ten or a dozen grand specimens.

Naturally with the numerous pools varying in size, depth and formation, no definite rule can be laid down as applicable to all, but some general principles should be borne in mind.

Taking a pool with a rocky overhang of about a foot, and with the water deep near the rock, but shallowing towards the sandy sides, place your net in the deepest part of the water under the rock, and gradually sweep in the direction of the shallows ; meanwhile keeping your net slightly tilted, so that the upper part of the frame scrapes the roof of the rock. The action should be firm and fairly quick. If nothing materialises, start again somewhere in the original position, and draw the net towards the other shallow end. Never work from the shallows to the deeps, as any potential victims would, if pursued in that way, have ample opportunity of making good their escape.

Many pools are bounded on one side by a rock which is cleft. In cases of that description do not push your net towards the division, and do not start to drag the pool from that area, as your efforts will be in vain. Instead, place your net, as far back as possible, in the fissure, and slide it outwards, keeping one side of the frame of the net hard up to the face of the rock, then round the rock, towards the sandy edge of the pool. Whether you are successful or not in your endeavour, try a further essay, this time from the same position in the fissure, but round to the other side of the pool.

When your net is in the water keep a sharp look out for any escaping prawns, as, if you notice some, you will be incited to work that pool again and again until you have captured them.

To remove the prawns from the net, place your hand over them, and gently gather them into your palm, then drop them into your bag.

To keep the prawns in good condition, place some wet seaweed in your creel or bag; the creatures will quickly settle down under this protection, and hours afterwards you will find them full of vigour.

CHAPTER XIII

WHERE TO PRAWN

PRAWNS are to be found on sandy shores, where they can obtain the shelter of plenty of friendly rocks. An open bay with a bed of sand which is destitute of rocks, is not the place to use your prawning net. You must have rocks and pools for you to follow your pastime. Those long and weed-covered reefs of flat rocks that stretch far out to sea, separated by wide bands of gleaming sand, constitute unmistakable evidence of the presence of prawns. Along those reefs you may expect to discover innumerable pools, some shallow and some deep, but the shallow ones provide the best places in which to ply your net. The deep ones, often containing big boulders, do not permit an effective movement of the net, with the consequence that the prawns can easily elude capture.

An area of low rocks, generously interspersed with patches of sand, also offers favourable opportunities to sample the resultant pools.

Usually in the vicinity of the rocky extents you will observe, floating in the sea, corks that denote the situation of lobster pots, and where lobsters are to be found, you may consider the neighbourhood as being propitious to prawns.

Although the prospects in some pools are obviously good, and in others certainly poor, do not, unless, by the making tide, you are pressed for time, turn down the unlikely ones without a test, as apart from the possibility of striking lucky, you will gain a lot in knowledge if you familiarise yourself with the singularities of the shore.

As an example of the spurned belying its apparent reputation I will recall an experience which happened to me some years ago.

With numerous other competitors I had worked a certain reef many times, and in the course of the journey, a small pool in the flat rock was passed on each trip. Like everybody else I ignored this pool because it was so insignificant and appeared to be too tiny to hold any life. It was square in shape, no more than a foot long and of similar width, with a depth of about three inches. Round the edges was a fringe of thick seaweed, and the pool's only virtue was to serve as a mark for pools of ample proportions nearer the sands.

One day, whilst waiting for the tide to fall sufficiently to allow of the customary waters to be drawn, I put my net into the disdained pool, purely out of idle curiosity, as there was scarcely room for the frame to take a horizontal position. Pushing the net against the weed I found that there was no opposition, and what I asumed to be a rocky side proved to be a chink. Standing up, I thought furiously, and with increasing interest, surveyed the pool critically, then, having picked the most suitable place from which to operate, I slid my net under the weed-covered projection. One foot, two feet, three feet of handle disappeared, and just as I was beginning to imagine that I should not reach the limit of the opening, I felt the rocky boundary obstructing the frame. After raising the net, I gently withdrew it, and when it reached daylight, the welcome clatter told its own story. I repeated the action from the other three sides of the pool, and when my task was finished, I had gathered over forty bulky prawns, and a lobster of a couple of pounds.

Ever since that memorable day I have never missed my special pool, and I have never been disappointed. Evidently the place is one favoured by the prawn family, and I can understand their choice, for in those secret and dark passages they are free from the attentions of their natural foes.

At dead low water, and just when the tide is about to turn, fair returns may often be enjoyed by working under the rocks washed by the creeping waves. Then, as the tide flows, try once again in the pools that you have already explored, as you will be surprised how much they have drained during your absence, and in the remaining waters you may catch some solitary rascals that evaded you on your earlier visits.

By the time that you have finished your round you will probably feel that your spoil has been well earned, for in literal terms you have, in your pursuit, had to " get down to it."

CHAPTER XIV

WHEN TO PRAWN

FROM May to September, inclusive, prawning from the shore can be undertaken with not only advantage, but with pleasure, as during those months the water is sufficiently warm in which to paddle without discomfort.

Concurrently with a new moon and a full moon the tides are both highest and lowest. In the course of the periods covered by the actual dates of these new and full moons, and for two or three days following respectively, long stretches of uncovered sands and reefs meet the eye when the tide has ebbed. Stretches that at other times are lost under many feet of surgy water. While the flatter the bed of the sea, the greater is the area that is exposed. Thus at intervals of a fortnight the opportunity occurs of putting the prawning net to good use, for then the prawns are trapped in the myriads of pools which are accessible only on those days. For about two hours, roughly an hour before and an hour after the turn to flow, endeavours can be made to fill the bag, and though the length of duration sounds generous, you will be astonished at the speedy passing of that time ; while you will also be surprised at the amount of ground that you traverse. A pool here, another not many yards away, several more a little farther distant, and so you progress from one to another, giving small heed to the ticking of the minutes, or to the distance that you journey.

Apart from a soaking wet day when the shore is out of the question, there are other climatic conditions which will frustrate your desires. If a very heavy sea has been running for a day there is not much hope of scoring a good count, while unseasonably cold water appears to keep the prawns off shore.

Again, if the sea is full of particles of broken seaweed, to work the clogged pools would be sheer waste of time and energy.

Undoubtedly the most advantageous time to register big totals is when the sea is calm, and when it has been nicely warmed by a summer's hot sun. Then, if you fail, you may depend that you have been robbed by some sea-borne marauders.

Though there are other means of catching prawns, the prawning net is, without question, synonymous of true sport, for to obtain the prey one has to hunt, and the real pleasure, probably, is aroused by the exercise of the necessary skill demanded. One grand feature of this sport is that no bait is required, and the follower has to rely only on a low tide, a net, and his own acumen.

Of the other methods employed, the most favoured, in certain districts, is the use of what is known as the hoop net. This is a simple contrivance composed of an iron hoop about two feet in diameter, and to which is attached a cord net some fifteen inches in depth. The hoop is suspended by

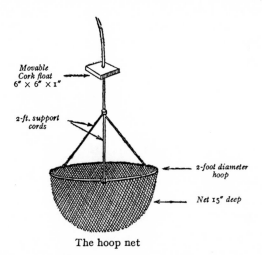

Movable
Cork float
6″ × 6″ × 1″

2-ft. support
cords

2-foot diameter
hoop

Net 15″ deep

The hoop net

three cords, each two feet in length, and these cords are connected with a rope the length of which depends, to some extent, upon the height of the rocks from the sea where the net is to be tried. Attached to the rope is a large cork that can be moved as required. Of course the measurements, which are those of a professional's gear, are not arbitrary, and a net of smaller dimensions may be constructed.

The *modus operandi* is to place a heavy stone in the net, together with some bait, and then to drop the net over the side of a suitable rock. The rock selected should be, as far as possible, one with a perpendicular side, so that the net can sink, without obstruction, to the bottom. When the depth of the water has been ascertained, the cork on the rope should be so adjusted as to permit the lower part of the net to rest near the sandy bed.

After an interval of about ten minutes the net is hauled up, and any imprisoned prawns withdrawn. If you are not rewarded, you should give the next immersion a longer spell, and if that is not productive, move to another position, as the set of the tide may be acting adversely.

Amateurs usually resort to green crabs, mussels and limpets, all smashed, for bait, but the professional needs something more odoriferous, and any remnants of fish offal—the more antique the better —will satisfy him.

If you wish to pursue this description of prawning, and long for a bag of large proportions, an excellent plan is to arm yourself with three or more nets. By that means you can keep yourself fully engaged. Bait and drop in number one net, and deal with the others similarly. When you have finished the lot, the time is nearly ripe to commence hauling, and the period at your disposal will quickly pass.

With the ordinary prawning net what you catch is not all in all : there is far more joy to be obtained than by the mere counting of the material gains. The sun and the breeze, the salt-laden air and the healthy exercise make a much greater total on the credit side at the end of your trip, than the actual number of prawns in your bag. Then think of the many interesting things that have come to your net, starfish and edible crabs, green crabs and spider crabs, baby pollock and wrasse of many hues, together with numerous varieties of tiny fish, some of which, perhaps later on, will give you a thrill when you are holding your rod.

Probably on your first venture with the prawning net you will be introduced to more mysteries of the deep than you have ever met previously. Then, as you wander back along the high-water mark, your eyes may pick out many insignificant treasures revealed by the spring-tide, including innumerable dainty shells, with here and there the ever popular cowrie waiting to be collected.

When you reach the pebbly bank, and sit down to change your shoes, perhaps the riches there may claim your attention. Amongst the piles of ordinary pebbles in infinite number you may detect crystals and agates, with an odd carnelian or amethyst, and for a few minutes you will forget any tiredness resulting from your earlier labours.

Though the wooded banks of stream and river are unsurpassed in natural glories, the seashore can, in its inimitable way, offer countless attractions to anyone willing to enjoy them.

Should you make up your mind to give a prawning net a trial, you may expect plenty of diversion, for while a man with a rod on the beach is a kind of target for passers-by, the man with a net is not complete without a gallery during the holiday season. Some of the onlookers may be quiescent in their curiosity, but others, no doubt, will allow their expectancy to override their prudence, in which case your presence in the pool will probably be augmented by others who unfortunately are too active. Still, it is all great fun, and if you can enjoy the humorous side of life, you will be thoroughly entertained.

Some of my most amusing experiences have been gained when, with a prawning net, I have embarked on the alluring adventure.

One day, not so many summers ago, a companion and I were awaiting for the ebbing tide to allow us to cross from a shore reef to one only approachable at very low water. Our venue contained many highly desirable pools, and the wait we knew was well worth the while. To pass the time away profitably, without loss of valuable minutes later on, we decided to sit on the rocks and eat our lunch. Being close on one o'clock the shore was almost deserted by the visitors, and as we ate, we contented ourselves with a little desultory conversation. Suddenly behind me a rather stentorian voice assailed me, " Well, my man, what are you after, whelks or cockles ? "

Turning round, I beheld a resplendent figure in immaculate white trousers perfectly creased, brown and white leather shoes, navy blue coat and vest, and an obviously new panama : all so painfully trim.

Before I had time to reply the owner of this glad garb continued, " I come from town, you know ; staying at the —— (mentioning an exceptionally expensive hotel), and I was wondering what your occupation is."

Tipping a wink to my companion I answered, " No, sir, we are not after whelks or cockles, simply prawns."

" Prawns : those brown things they call shrimps ? "

" Oh, no, prawns ; they are pink when they are cooked, and if you drop into ——'s (naming a famous restaurant in town) you will see them there."

"——'s. Good gracious, fancy hearing that place spoken of in this outlandish part of the country ! Shouldn't have thought that you had ever heard of the place. Well, I must toddle off or I'll miss the gong."

When our interviewer had departed, my companion burst our laughing, and said, " You were pretty mild with the pompous old bean."

" Oh, I don't know. You see, he is down here thinking that he is giving us a treat, so we must be tolerant."

Later in the afternoon when our expedition had ended, and I had reached the parade where my car was parked, he of the immaculate white trousers espied me, and joining me, remarked, " Well, my good man, did you catch any of those things ? "

Since referring to ——'s Restaurant I had evidently risen in his estimation, I thought, as I was promoted to being his " good " man.

" Yes, sir, quite a nice lot, somewhere about a hundred."

" And what are you going to do with them ? Take them to the fishmonger's, I suppose, and sell them."

" No," I answered pleasantly, " I am taking them home, and I hope that my family will enjoy them for tea."

Reaching my car, I discarded my wet, well-worn jacket, and after donning one more presentable, took the wheel.

As I drove off, I waved my hand to the imperious one, but his returned salute appeared to be a trifle half-hearted, and I thought that he looked a little crestfallen.

Yes, there is a lot of fun to be had on the seashore, great fun ; so come along and join the jolly party of anglers and prawners.

THE END

INDEX

A

Agate End Ring, 31, 32
Allcocks " Little Witch "
Spinner, 25
Angling Associations, 42
Angling Publications, 95

B

Bait, 20, 26, 41, 42, 44, 45,
46, 48, 49, 82, 83, 85,
86, 96, 118
Bloater, 48
Cockles, 48
Crabs, 41, 42, 85, 118
Herring, 48
King Rag, 46
Kipper, 48
Limpets, 118
Lug-worms, 44
Mackerel, 46, 82
Mussel, 49
Prawns, 49, 96
Rag-worms, 45, 83, 86
Spider Crab, 49
Squid, 49
Bakelite Reel, 33
Bass, 19, 22, 26, 34, 35, 51,
58, 62, 63, 66, 73, 74,
78, 79, 82, 84

Bass Hooks, 34, 35
Bell, 56
Bites, 57
Bloater, 48
Box Brass Swivels, 36, 79,
80, 90
Brill, 23

C

Care of Tackle, 88
Casting, 50
Casting stance, 53
Casts, 34, 35, 36, 78, 80, 90
Climatic Conditions, 75, 76,
77
Cloudy Days, 75
Cockles, 48
Cod, 24
Codling, 24
Conger, 26
Cooking Prawns, 105
Crabs, 41, 42, 85, 118

D

Dabs, 23
Disgorger, 39, 91
Dog-fish, 19, 25
" Durofix," 89

INDEX

124

Printed in the United Kingdom
by Lightning Source UK Ltd.
131592UK00001B/151/A